Use Time

Or It Will Use You

R. Geoff Dromey

Griffith University

What we lack more than anything else is time.
-- Michelle Fitoussi

2nd Edition
**Published 2012 by Systems & Software Quality Institute Pty. Ltd.
Edited by David Tuffley.**
www.ssqi.org.au/
ISBN-13: 978-1468171136   ISBN-10: 1468171135

Copyright © The R. Geoff Dromey Estate, 1997 - 2012.
All rights reserved. Without limiting the rights under copyright reserved above, no part of this publication may be reproduced, stored in, or introduced into a retrieval system, or transmitted, in any form without the prior written permission of the copyright owner.

About the Author
Professor R. Geoff Dromey was the Foundation Professor of Software Engineering in the School of Information and Communication Technology at Griffith University in Brisbane, Australia. He was the founder and Director of the Software Quality Institute at Griffith University.

Profits from the sale of this book will go to the *Professor R. Geoff Dromey Foundation and Scholarship Fund* to facilitate industry focused applied academic research to advance and improve systems and software engineering capability.

Contents

PREFACE (READ FIRST) 1
WAYS TO USE THIS BOOK 2
CHAPTER 1: THE STRATEGIC USE OF TIME 4
   WE DO NOT HAVE ENOUGH TIME 4
   WHAT TIME MEANS TO US 5
   IT IS WHAT WE DO WITH TIME THAT COUNTS 9
   WHAT WE ALL SEEK 10
   WHAT SOCIETY VALUES 12
   BREAKING THROUGH THE TIME BARRIER 13
   INVESTING TIME IN WHAT IS IMPORTANT 16
   DEVELOPING TIME-SKILLS 17
CHAPTER 2: LAWS OF TIME INVESTMENT 20
   CREATING AN ABUNDANCE OF TIME 20
   LAW 1: CREATE AND MAINTAIN A COMPELLING FUTURE 21
   LAW 2: INVEST TIME IN YOUR FUTURE 24
   LAW 3: INVEST TIME IN WORTHY GOALS 26
   LAW 4: TIME MUST BE MADE FOR IMPORTANT THINGS 28
   LAW 5: INVEST TIME IN PERSONAL GROWTH 29
   LAW 6: INVEST TIME IN OTHER PEOPLE 30
   LAW 7: FOCUS ON THE VITAL FEW (PARETO PRINCIPLE) 34
   LAW 8: THE LAST 20% MAKES THE DIFFERENCE 35
   LAW 9: WORTHY RESULTS TAKE TIME 37
   LAW 10: AVOID USELESS ACTIVITY 37
   LAW 11: DO NOT DWELL ON ACHIEVEMENT, THE PAST OR FAILURE .. 38
CHAPTER 3: LAWS OF TIME UTILIZATION 40
   MAKING EFFECTIVE USE OF OUR TIME 40
   LAW 1: VALUE YOUR TIME 41
   LAW 2: LET THE GOAL BE THE GUIDE 42
   LAW 3: PRIORITIZE YOUR USE OF TIME 44
   LAW 4: PLAN YOUR TIME 46
   LAW 5: STICK TO YOUR PRIORITIES AND PLANS 49
   LAW 6: GUARD YOUR TIME 50
   LAW 7: MEASURE YOUR USE OF TIME 51
   LAW 8: USE AN EFFECTIVE PROCESS 54

Contents

LAW 9: AVOID FREQUENT TASK-SWITCHING 56
LAW 10: DON'T JUST TWIDDLE YOUR THUMBS AT ROAD-BLOCKS 62
LAW 11: EXPEND THE TIME REQUIRED 63
LAW 12: ACCOMPLISH ALL YOU CAN 65
LAW 13: INVEST AT THE RIGHT TIME 67
LAW 14: INVEST THE RIGHT AMOUNT OF TIME 68
LAW 15: COMPOSE ACTIVITIES WISELY 70

CHAPTER 4: MANAGING THE USE OF TIME 73

WHY OUR USE OF TIME SHOULD BE MANAGED 73
WHAT MANAGING TIME ENTAILS 74
PLANNING AND MEASUREMENT OF TIME 75
IMPROVING YOUR UTILIZATION OF TIME 82
ROLE OF HABITS IN IMPROVING TIME SKILLS 83
BREAKING BAD HABITS -BUILDING GOOD HABITS 84
TIME UTILIZATION MATURITY MODEL 86
  Level 1: Chaotic 88
  Level 2: Immature 89
  Level 3: Defined 91
  Level 4: Managed 92
  Level 5: Optimizing 93

CHAPTER 5: OPTIMIZING THE USE OF TIME 95

KIPLING'S PROFOUND ADVICE 95
ASSESSING THE WORTHINESS OF GOALS 96
  Motivation 96
  Significance of goal 97
  Cost and benefits 97
  Long-lasting value 98
ON BEING *INVOLVED* IN WHAT WE ARE DOING 98
DOING THINGS WE DON'T FEEL LIKE DOING 101
MAINTAINING MOMENTUM ON LONG PROJECTS 103
  Threats to projects 104
  Keeping projects on track 106
IMPROVING THE WAY WE DO THINGS 108
  Improvement framework 109
ACCOMPLISHING A LOT IN A SHORT TIME 113
  Planning 114
  Doing 114
  Having the energy to get the job done 115
  Creating the right working environment 116

Contents

SMELLING THE ROSES ALONG THE WAY 117
LIVING AN IDEAL DAY EVERY DAY 119
CHAPTER 6: TIME AND YOUR FUTURE **124**
CHAPTER 7: A PLAN FOR ACTION **128**
   WHERE DO WE START? 128
   ACTION PLAN 129
      Quality of life planning *130*
      Strategic questions *132*
      Time skills improvement plan *133*
   DAILY PLANNING PROCESS 137
      Things to keep in mind each day *140*
   WEEKLY PLANNING PROCESS 141
   MONTHLY PLANNING PROCESS 142
   HALF-YEARLY REVIEW AND ANNUAL PLANNING 143
   A PLAN FOR ACTION 145
      1. Review laws of time investment, utilisation *145*
      2. Determine your medium & long-term goals *147*
      3a. Determine quality of life improvements *148*
      3b. Determine goals & milestones *149*
      4. Determine your Time Utilisation Maturity *150*
      5. Determine your time-wasting habits *155*
      6. Use your TIME-table *156*
APPENDIX I: PROBLEMS WITH OUR USE OF TIME **158**
   WHY DO WE WASTE TIME? 158
   WHY DO WE FAIL TO PLAN? 159
   WHY DO WE PUT THINGS OFF? 162
   WHY DO WE ALWAYS FEEL BUSY? 165
   WHY DO WE OVERWORK? 166
   WHY DON'T WE GIVE IMPORTANT THINGS HIGHEST PRIORITY? 168
   WHY DO WE TAKE TOO LONG TO COMPLETE TASKS? 170
   WHY DO PEOPLE GIVE UP ON WORTHWHILE PROJECTS? 173
   WHY DO WE GET BORED? 176
   CAN WE BE HAPPY DOING "NOTHING"? 178
APPENDIX II: THE PSYCHOLOGY OF TIME UTILIZATION .. **180**
   WHAT INFLUENCES OUR BEHAVIOUR? 180
   THE ROLE OF HABITS IN TIME UTILIZATION 185
   INFLUENCES WORKING AGAINST OUR EFFECTIVE USE OF TIME 189

Contents

INFLUENCES ENCOURAGING US TO USE OUR TIME EFFECTIVELY..... 191
THE WAY AHEAD 192

Preface (Read First)

This book has a different focus from others that have been written on the human use of time. It is designed to inspire, to motivate and to assist *anyone and everyone who is interested in improving the quality of their life.*

The greatest pleasure and satisfaction in life comes from the accomplishment of things that require large investments of time. In a nutshell, this book is about how to create that *abundance of time* that you need to invest to realize your long-term goals and ambitions.

Each and every one of us has a great untapped potential to use our time much more effectively. If we exploit this potential we can accomplish things that will make our lives richer, make the world a better place, and give pleasure and inspiration to those we love and touch.

Most authors hope that their books will be read and appreciated. If that is all this book does for you, it will have failed. My hope for this book is twofold: first, that it will make you *think*, and second, it will cause you to *take action.*

Geoff Dromey,
Griffith University,
Brisbane, 1997.

Ways to use this book

Each of us has different backgrounds and different needs. Consequently the way we set about getting what we want from a book can differ considerably.

Every author hopes that readers will read all that they have written, preferably in the order in which it is presented. However this is not the way the world works, or the way people necessarily behave.

To accommodate people who are "busy" the book has been kept deliberately short. This is a carrot to encourage people to read the whole thing. Readers who just want to get to the main game as quickly as possible often run the risk of getting a distorted and incomplete view of what a book offers. Also, by being focussed only on what to do, a reader runs the risk of missing important motivating arguments designed to keep them committed to improving their time-skills. Without this backup they may lose interest before they have derived real benefits from improving their time-skills. Things worth having, and of lasting value, don't just happen overnight. If you think any book on time utilization is going to deliver you the magic formula in a single cursory reading of a couple of chapters you are likely to be disappointed. This book can offer a lot to help you improve your time-skills, provided you are not in too much of a rush to get the results before you have done the ground work and paid your dues. For those who think they do not have time to read the whole book the following advice is offered.

Use time or it will use you

The Reader Who Knows a Lot About The Subject and Who Is Looking To See If This Book Has Anything New To Say

Readers in this category should at least read Chapter 1 to get a perspective on what the book is trying to do. Chapters 2 and 3 deserve at least a quick visit to see what the laws offer. Chapters 4, 5 and 7 should be of most interest to readers in this category. They may find Appendices I and II discussing problems they are already well aware of.

The Reader Who Just Wants To Know What To Do And How To Do It Without Worrying About Why

This reader, who just wants to get hold of, and start applying the technology as quickly as possible, should at least read chapter 1 and then chapter 7 followed by chapter 4. This way of getting what you want from the book may work for some people. My personal feeling is that a reader who opts to do this, will lack the background, motivation and the perspective to maximize the benefits that they could obtain from the book.

The Author's Model Reader

This reader will read what has been written with an open mind, but in a critical and reflective way. They will weigh up what is said, and take away from the book what is useful to them. This reader will be prepared to try out things, to take action and to see what really works for them. Readers in this category will find it useful to read Appendices I and II straight after Chapter 1 in order to gain a better understanding of the *problem* before getting caught up in the "how to".

Chapter 1:
The strategic use of time

Our quality-of-life in the future depends upon the quality of our thinking (and actions) in the present -- Edward de Bono

We do not have enough time

In today's fast-paced world so many of us experience the feeling of not having enough time to do the things that are important to us, the things we would dearly love to do and even the things we have to do. There is that ever-present feeling of being under pressure or having too much to do. No matter what we try, or how hard we work, there is no light at the end of the tunnel. Our quality-of-life is far from what we want it to be.

Over the past five hundred years the human race has made giant strides in education, in science and in the use of labour-saving technology. *However, by any of these yardsticks, the way we handle time is still in the dark ages.* All around us people are living in dire time poverty.

Take even this short book. Unless you belong to a small minority, it won't be easy for you to find the time to read it. This situation would change little even if you believed the book could be of great benefit to you. Here, right before your eyes, at this very moment, your lack of time is confronting you and limiting you! Most people don't get past the first ten pages of any book. Other seemingly more pressing things demand their attention or distract them and consume their time.

An endless stream of demands on our time keep rolling in from all quarters. There is little time to focus and to concentrate. We struggle to make any real progress on the things that are important to us. Instead of being active users of time, we find that others, and external events beyond our control, always seem to be dictating how we spend our time. Days pass, months pass and even years can pass, without anything very satisfying being accomplished? We are too busy reacting to things to pay serious attention to strategically and effectively using our time.

There is a way out. You can escape this *time poverty* by learning and **actively using** an effective set of *time skills* like those described in this book. Superior time skills will give you the freedom you need to realize your full potential and to change, forever, your quality of life.

Use Time or It Will Use You Chapter 1: The Strategic Use Of Time

What time means to us

We regard life as precious and go to great lengths to preserve it. Rarely however, do we extend this belief to what should be its logical consequence -that of placing an equally high value on how we use our time.

Why should we bother to do this? The answer is simple - what we do with our time affects the quality of our life *now*, and in the *future*. This consequence is inescapable.

Time is the most precious resource any of us has.

Only when we come to see time in this light are we likely to start using it to improve our quality-of-life.

Like all valuable resources, there are many things we can do with time. We may waste it, abuse it, ignore it, spend it, value it, save it, and even take the enlightened step of investing it. The eminent inventor Benjamin Franklin once said: *time is money*. With all due respect to Franklin, this assessment of time is too limiting and unadventurous. If he had said: **time is opportunity**, he would have given us far better advice. Time is the key resource we all must use to improve the way we live.

Regardless of anything else, there are four fundamental things that have a long-lasting impact on our quality-of-life:

- the long-term goals we accomplish
- our continuing personal growth
- our commitment to those close to us and to society,
- our health and fitness

Our seeming lack of time prevents most of us from striking the balance among these factors that would make us truly happy. If we get this balance right, it is possible to be happy and relaxed, and still accomplish far more than most. Not only can we do this, but more importantly, we can do it without the pressure of being constantly busy and without working exceptionally hard. What it comes down to, is how we choose to invest our time.

While the major focus in the rest of this book is upon using time strategically to achieve long-term goals, we take it as given that the set of long-term goals we choose should always include as high priorities the other three things (i.e., personal growth, health and fitness, etc) we have spelled out which give quality to our life.

This is something we should not compromise on, no matter what our current circumstances or what our past has been, if we want to live life to the full and achieve what will give us long-lasting pleasure and satisfaction.

The tetrahedron below, which succinctly summarizes this philosophy and emphasizes three things:

- the importance of *balance* between the four factors,
- that all of these factors *contribute equally* to our quality-of-life, and
- that each factor is *supported and reinforced* by the other three.

When you achieve balance between these elements, leading to an improved quality of life, you will find that an increasing synergy comes about.

Synergy is when the total or the whole is more than the sum of the parts. It is seen in fully optimising people, a person who is moving towards a state of self-actualisation. Such a state is natural, representing your fullest potential as a human being.

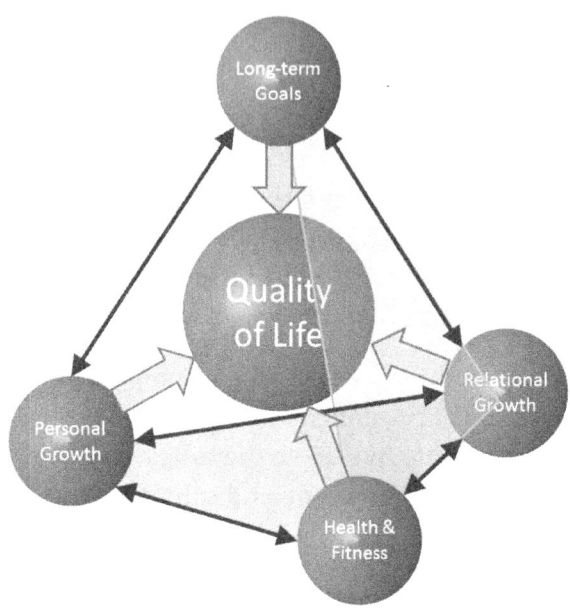

This structure maps in a natural way onto our reality. It captures in an essence, what life could be, or perhaps even what life should be all about. Each factor supports the other three. Just as the geometric structure is highly stable, so too should be a life that is lived and balanced according to these factors.

If we fail to develop one or more of these dimensions we will pay a price which is measured by a corresponding loss in the quality of our life. When we look around us we see manifestations of all these possibilities. There are people who excel in all dimensions, right through to people who excel in only one dimension at the expense of the others. Finally there are some who do not excel in any of these dimensions.

There is always plenty of scope for each and everyone of us to extend and balance our growth along these dimensions. If we can do this, we will achieve a marked improvement in our quality-of-life.

For most of us, of the four dimensions, the achievement of long-term goals is the one which is most often neglected. It is also the one that is most difficult to accomplish -hence the focus on long-term goals in this book. By long-term goals here we mean things that are likely to take us six months, a year, two years, or even much longer to achieve.

It is what we do with time that counts

When all the dust is cleared away it is not time itself that is of much consequence -it is what we *do* with our time that really counts. People do not pay serious attention to time because they fail to appreciate what it *could* do for them if they were to learn to use it strategically and effectively.

What each of us does with our time makes a very big difference to the quality of the life we experience, what we accomplish, and our future.

We claim that what we do with time, more than anything else, has a profound effect on the quality of our lives. This raises a very fundamental issue -*do we each place enough importance on the way we live, and on what we achieve?* If we do, then time should be very important to us. It is the primary resource we use to do *absolutely everything*. Let us put the issue another way. When we ask people if their *quality-of-life* is important to them, we get a unanimous "yes". We therefore owe it to ourselves to understand why time is, or should be, important to us.

What we all seek

In living, we seek *pleasure* and *satisfaction* from what we do. Taken together, pleasure and satisfaction add up to *happiness*. Throughout this book, we intend to use the words pleasure and satisfaction in quite distinct ways. On the one hand we will associate pleasure with our own feelings about what we do, what we experience, and what we accomplish. On the other hand, we will associate satisfaction with our feelings about what we perceive or project that other people think about our actions or accomplishments.

Peoples' motives for what ever they do are to seek pleasure and satisfaction and/or avoid pain.

There are countless things we can do that give pleasure and satisfaction. However, the degree of lasting satisfaction, pleasure or benefit we get from what we do seems to be intimately tied to the scale, or size, or difficulty of the task or accomplishment. For example, to win an Olympic Gold Medal might only take a few seconds or minutes. However, almost invariably, years of effort and training goes into reaching the level where winning such a medal is even a remote possibility.

In contrast to this, sitting down and watching a movie for a couple of hours gives us pleasure. The catch is, that the feeling of pleasure derived from this very passive action rarely lasts much beyond the time it takes to watch the movie. In other words, it is a very transitory pleasure. There will be very few people who will come up to you on the street and congratulate you for having spent the time to watch a particular movie. The personal payoff for this sort of activity is very small. It passes the time, that is all.

So what we see here is that winning an Olympic Gold Medal and watching a movie both take time; what is involved, and what are the outcomes in the respective cases, in terms of pleasure and satisfaction, are however, worlds apart. Analysing these two situations, we see that there are at least a few people who are prepared to forego a lot of transitory pleasure and maybe even endure considerable pain and hardship to realize long-lasting pleasure and satisfaction. On the other hand, a much larger group of people seek, or only ever attain transitory pleasure. There is a place for transitory pleasure but it is unlikely that seeking just transitory pleasure will make us truly happy. *Each and every one of us has the capacity to do things that would change our lives, that would change the way we think about ourselves and would change the way other people think about us. The opportunity is there for us to seize.*

The preceding discussion would seem to suggest that small things that only involve small investments of time are not of much long-term consequence. We should be wary about jumping too quickly to such a conclusion. There are many "little things" we can do that can have a lasting positive impact on our life and on the lives of others. These "little things" are usually things that are done spontaneously and selflessly without any thought of recognition or reward. One prime example of this is unconditionally giving a little of your time and undivided attention to another person. By giving, in fact you usually receive far more pleasure and satisfaction in return.

There is yet another dimension to what people seek -that is, the avoidance of a feeling we usually loosely describe as pain. In some instances, avoiding pain is a stronger influence on our behaviour than the desire for pleasure and satisfaction. In fact, pain often stops us from doing lots of things because they involve some risk of failure, hardship or embarrassment. A voiding, putting off, or choosing not to do certain things often has two possible consequences. It leads to the creation of a worse situation which in the end wastes or costs us a lot more unnecessary time and pain than if we had confronted the issue in the first place. Alternatively, it can result in missed opportunities which could have made a significant difference to our situation and to the quality of our life.

What society values

There are two clear messages that flow from our preceding discussion. What our peers and what society seems to value, applaud, and recognize most in others, are things that take a lot of effort, skill, persistence and time to accomplish. And, what individuals usually derive the greatest lasting pleasure, satisfaction and benefit from are those same things that involve very substantial effort to accomplish. Steve Jobs, co-founder of Apple Computer, summed this up very nicely when he said: "Most things I've done take many years . . . I'm always impatient but it doesn't speed things up."

Society values achievement because people know that a large amount of effort must have gone into its realization. Part of this recognition often stems from the fact that people acknowledge that they, themselves would not have the strength of character, energy and persistence to achieve such a goal. They also recognize that people who achieve long-term goals, unlike themselves, have had to forego lots of transitory pleasure in order to realize their achievements.

The other main reason why society values the achievement of long-term goals is because such achievements often make the world a better place in some way. Take the case of the inventor Thomas Edison who persisted for so long time before finally identifying a suitable material from which to make light bulbs. His persistence and achievement has ensured that he will always have a place in history.

Breaking through the time barrier

It is our lack of time, like an insurmountable barrier, that is always standing there before us preventing us from doing so many of the things we want to do -things which we know we are capable of doing.

More people would try to, and be able to achieve, fulfilling and exciting long-term goals if they only knew how to more effectively use their time.

If we are to break through this barrier and find the time we need to do the things we really want to do then there are a number of changes we will need to make in our attitudes and in our behavior. This is not something that will happen over night even when we understand what needs to be done. It will only happen if we invest the time and the sustained effort to make the changes. A fundamental law operates here -it says *you only get out of things a return that is commensurate with the effort that you put in, in the first place.* No one is going to deliver you more time on a plate. You can certainly gain access to a lot more time but you are going to have to earn it through your own efforts.

Many of us put off doing things that we want to do, and things that are important to us, because we have the forlorn hope that somehow in the future we will have more time to do these things. This is just wishful thinking. The chances of it happening are usually remote. We have to make the tough decision to MAKE time now to fit in the things that are important us. This means allocating and spending time each and every day on these things we really want to do. We will only succeed if we hold firmly to this. Compromises and disruptions to our commitment should be few and far between.

Your response to this suggestion might be -well that is unrealistic or impossible with the schedule and commitments that I have. If this is your response then you should reassess your priorities. Most of us try to hide behind the excuse that we are already too busy. Being "busy" is a situation we need to send packing out of our life very quickly. There are always more things that we could do or that we think we have to do, than there is time for. This situation is quite normal. It certainly does not constitute a legitimate excuse for putting off important things that we really want to do. All it usually means is that we have let things come rolling in on top of us without giving enough thought to prioritization and to sorting out what is really important to our long-term happiness.

We must reject completely, now and forever, the notion that we are too busy.

We need to recognize that there are always choices regarding how we use our time. Our job is to make the choices and devote time to things according to their importance and long-term impact on our lives. If we do this we will cease to be busy and start being effective. I know, in my own case, since I have stopped saying or believing that I am "busy" there has been a change as dramatic as the contrast between night and day. I am doing as many, if not more things than before; the difference is, I no longer feel stressed. And, as a bonus, I am also getting a lot more of what really counts, done.

Our lack of skill in investing time wisely and in using time effectively, contribute in a major way to the barrier that prevents most of us from ever achieving substantial goals that would make a real difference to the quality of our lives. So many more people have the talent to achieve worthwhile goals than ever achieve such goals. They either never start, because they cannot see how they will find the time to accomplish the task, or they start, but because of their poor use of time, they stall and give up long before their goal is anywhere in sight.

To set the right preconditions for breaking through the "lack-of-time barrier" we must add to our mind-set the recognition that time is our most valuable resource. It then becomes much easier to make the switch to actively and strategically investing our time each and every day.

Investing time in what is important

Time, like money, must be invested in substantial amounts to accomplish things of value. Investing substantial amounts of time regularly, over a long period to accomplish a task, or achieve a goal, is not something that can be done lightly, if it is to be effective. Very few people naturally and intuitively have the ability to do this.

To achieve long-term goals we certainly cannot go about things in a half-hearted or half-baked way. We have to make a commitment, we have to be involved, and we have to be passionate about what we want to achieve. This must be coupled with a commitment to master how to make time and how to invest time if we are to give ourselves a chance of accomplishing long-term and worthwhile goals.

Disciplined investment of time is what is needed to achieve long-term goals and attain lasting pleasure and satisfaction.

While this all sounds good in theory it is also important to recognise that investment of time is a skill that must be nurtured and developed as a very strategic activity over a considerable period. It can be hard to break old habits and equally hard to establish new, worthwhile time habits. It is alright to be impatient for, and hopeful of, immediate large-scale improvement. However, do not be surprised if the gains you are seeking come more slowly. Keep in mind that a one percent daily improvement will lead to a doubling in performance in approximately three months. Time is on your side when persistence is your ally.

Developing time-skills

Making the commitment to develop your time-skills will be one of the most important decisions you make in your life if you have the patience and persistence to follow it through to fruition. It will change forever your quality-of-life.

Despite the potential benefits of having effective time-skills, very few people ever seriously venture into this territory. That society, and the education system, overlooks such a critical life-skill is a great pity. Its consequence is a great waste in human potential and a loss of happiness. Not only would individuals benefit and be happier from having better time-skills, but society in general, would also be the winner.

Desire and commitment is not enough. People must learn through sustained practice how to use their time, just as they must learn how to walk, or swim, or any other skill. Very few people have jumped into the water for the first time and swam with the grace and power of a competent swimmer, let alone an Olympic Champion -the same applies to the effective use of time. Unfortunately, very few people understand or have ever thought about this. They just battle on doing things without recognizing that they need to diligently invest time and effort to develop their time-skills.

The ability to effectively use time is a skill that can only be mastered by diligent and sustained practise.

To master how to use our time strategically we need to have an overall plan for how we are going to improve our use of time. This plan must be underpinned by a philosophy and a set of perspectives, strategies and techniques that will help us to invest our time wisely and to use it effectively. Then we must carry out our plan and measure how well we perform relative to our targets. All of this, and more, is needed to substantially improve our effective use of time. The rest of this book addresses these issues.

What is presented should be of interest to a very wide audience; from professionals, to people in business, to students, to athletes in training, to people with hobbies, to parents with young children. The techniques can be used by people to achieve important things either as part of, or outside, their normal work or everyday activities. How you choose to use these techniques is a judgement you will need to make. Keep in mind that there are **168 hours in every week** -which is a lot of time. It should be possible for each and everyone of us to find, at the very least, 10% of this time to invest strategically, on a regular basis, in one or more worthy projects or goals that will make a significant difference to the quality of our life.

While the whole focus of what is presented is addressed to individuals, there is absolutely no reason why it should not

Use time or it will use you

deliver similar payoffs to teams and even larger organizations and bureaucracies -*the same laws of time investment and utilization apply on a collective scale, provided they are accompanied by a shared vision and a shared set of values and long-term goals.*

Chapter 2:
Laws of time investment

Wisdom lies in the intelligent perception of great principles and not in the slavish imitation of detail. E. Bramah

Creating an abundance of time

More than seventy years ago a little book titled "The Richest Man In Babylon" was published by George Clason. That book, which has been labelled the *most inspiring book on wealth ever written*, contained a lot of sound advice about how to accumulate and manage another precious resource -gold (wealth). The high-level guiding principles enunciated in that book were summarized in Clason's, Five Laws of Gold. Perhaps, not surprisingly, since time is also a precious resource, it too has a similar set of laws that govern its wise investment and effective utilization. Lasting pleasure and satisfaction is the gold we acquire in this case

While acquiring and managing wealth is an aim that appeals to some their is something else that has far greater appeal -to be happy, and to live life to the full. The problem is, to be truly happy and satisfied in life, we need to achieve long-term goals that require large investments of time and large investments of physical, emotional and/or mental effort to accomplish. Unfortunately, most people do not know how to create the abundance of time that they need to invest to achieve their long-term goals. The aim here is to put forward practical principles and strategies that may be used to create that abundance of time.

To achieve our long-term goals we must find time in our day-to-day routine that was previously wasted or used for other less important things. We will now enunciate a set of laws and provide a brief commentary on each one before considering the more practical aspects of investing and using time. The laws provided give clues on how to create a wealth of time in three ways:

- by investing it wisely
- by not doing some things, and
- by saving time doing other things.

Law 1: Create and maintain a compelling future

For each and everyone one of us, life is a journey through time. Wherever we happen to be on that journey, there is always a choice of directions, roads to travel and destinations to seek. The destinations within our sight, from our current vantage point, are always defined by the clarity of our vision. Many people ignore this by metaphorically turning their backs on the future. They stumble through life as if there were no horizons, no future, no destinations beyond what today offers. They never see possible interesting and challenging futures, things that they could accomplish, different styles of living they could create and ways in which they could contribute to improving the lot of humanity. Instead, the choices they make are dictated solely by the moment, by their current circumstances. Roman philosopher Seneca, captured this approach to living when he said: if you know not what harbour you are sailing jor, any wind is the right one. Is this the best way to live life? Surely not. Each and everyone of us owes it to ourselves, and to the rest of humanity, past, present and future, to try to do our part to create a better world, a better place to live and share our experiences, a better future for us all.

If, as we journey through time, we are constantly learning and growing, if we accomplishing new things, and if we are contributing to society, we will discover that the territory keeps changing and new destinations come within our sight and within our range. These opportunities are there to be seized, not ignored.

What we are talking about here is making some compelling choices about how to live. In creating a vision we need to make some tangible specifications about three things:

- *What we want to be,*
- *What we want to accomplish, and*
- *What we want to contribute*

A compelling vision gives us direction. It can also transform our life and give it real purpose and meaning. Of course, as we progress, and as we accomplish things our vision will change as new things become important.

Without meaningful personal long-term goals our life lacks direction, purpose and focus. And, as a consequence, it suffers in vitality and quality. Goals are important not only for what they will deliver when they are accomplished but also for improving the quality of our living along the way. A life lived without strong purpose is only half lived.

Deciding what that purpose is, and then committing to it, gives meaning to our life. There can be little quality in a life lived without purpose.

Some time ago I remember reading an article about survival in the Nazi Concentration Camps during World War II. The thrust of the article suggested that those who were most likely to survive were people who had a strong sense of purpose. They were people passionate about the things they wanted to accomplish when they got out of the mess they were in. These were people who had a powerful vision beyond their current circumstances, who had a compelling future. Few of us today face circumstances that could be even remotely linked to what those people experienced. We have no excuse for not creating a compelling future for ourselves.

The trees in the forest have something to teach us about how to live our lives. As a tree journeys through time it grows in grace and stature. It is always changing, renewing itself and adapting to its environment. It encounters hard seasons, which it accommodates, and good seasons in which it flourishes. Its roots (c.f. our values) are the key to its well-being. They nourish its growth, and give it the strength and stability to adapt to its changing environment. A tree's growth takes place in a number of different directions, but always with a view to maintaining its balance and the integrity of its structure. A tree is also always mindful of its environment and its relationships with its neighbours. It does not try to harm or take advantage of them. Instead, a tree does its best to play its part in creating a harmonious environment in which it, and all of its neighbours, can flourish. It helps protect its neighbours from strong winds and at the same time enjoys the protection and support that they in return provide. It is true that a tree competes with other trees for the light, for the space and the nutrients in the ground but it never seeks to do things in excess or take more than its fair share of resources.

There are always dangers in taking any analogy too far. People differ from trees in a myriad of ways. However, the tree-in-the-forest analogy gives us a number of things to reflect upon in choosing how to live.

Reading Theodore Zeldin's beautiful book, *An Intimate History of Humanity*, brings home just how easy it is for us to let our circumstances limit our vision, limit what we do, and dictate the quality and direction of our lives. Do we really have to repeat the mistakes of our ancestors, of our parents and of many of those we see around us. Should we opt for playing out roles that are largely predictable, unimaginative and unfulfilling? Need this be what we are prepared to accept, assuming we get only one chance at life?

Law 2: Invest time in your future

Clearly, how we spend our time, at all times, strongly influences the quality of our life now, and in the future. By wisely investing our time we can fulfil our ever-present needs for pleasure and satisfaction.

Accomplishment, success and satisfaction comes to those who invest at least 10% of every day working towards the achievement of long-term personal goals.

What this law is suggesting is that each and every one of us needs to have long-term personal goals that we are working towards on a consistent and regular basis. The claim is made that if, over a long period of time, we invest nearly two to three hours every day on worthy long-term goals we will realize accomplishments that will give us long-lasting pleasure and satisfaction. The force behind this principle of investment of time is exactly the same force that operates when money is invested. We know that when money is invested regularly for long periods it accumulates at an exponential rate. A similar sort of favourable return flows from regularly investing time on long-term goals over a long period of time. The challenge to find two or even three hours each day should not be too hard -for example, the average person spends roughly 25 hours per week (that is, three working-day equivalents) watching TV.

There is an important corollary to the law of regularly investing time in our future. What it says is that once we commit to working on a project or achieving a particular goal we should continue making regular (preferably daily) time commitments to that goal until it is achieved. When we do this we build up substantial momentum that ensures that we get the best return (as measured by progress) on our regular investments of time. In this sense, the law of investment of time works in a similar way to the law of investment of money. Investing relatively small amounts regularly, over a long time, in the end gives greater returns than sporadic intense efforts or fragmented efforts. What is more, we can achieve our goals without great sacrifice to our quality of life along the way.

Momentum, through regular, uninterrupted time investments is the key to almost effortlessly realizing long-term goals.

If, on the other hand, our investments of time towards achieving a goal are irregular or there are significant gaps between bursts of activity then much of the time that we invest gets lost along the way. It takes a lot more effort to restart a project after a break than to keep it bobbing along on a regular basis. In my own experience, this has been one of the most valuable lessons I have learned about the use of time. Projects carried out through regular uninterrupted time commitments are a pleasure to work on. Their realization appears before our eyes, almost without our noticing. It is a wonderful feeling. We feel at ease, we feel relaxed, but the project continues to role on towards its completion almost effortlessly. This is such a contrast to the way most large projects are brought to fruition. The sense of frustration, or strain or pressure that usually comes with the territory is gone.

Law 3: Invest time in worthy goals

Simply investing time to achieve goals is not enough. If we were investing our money we would take great care in selecting an investment. The same care should be exercised in investing time. We need to be strategic and highly selective in the choice of goals we choose to pursue.

Those who invest time in worthwhile long-term projects are rewarded

Each of us has our own idea of what constitutes a worthy goal. Our values, our needs and the influence of our peers and those close to us largely determine what we see as a worthy goal. Pushkin's advice is probably the best universal guide. He said: never compromise for glory or gain.

Before investing a lot of time to achieve any goal it is wise to bring to bear the best relevant information. To do this we need to use a set of criteria and an accompanying process to assess the "worthiness" of the goal. A series of questions which help determine:

- the significance of achieving the goal,
- what it will cost in effort and time,
- our level of motivation to accomplish it, and
- whether it is congruent with our core values.

These questions should be used to make the assessment. Details for doing this are provided in Chapter 5, which discusses optimising our use of time.

Law 4: Time must be made for important things

If we take the attitude that we will spend time working on important long-term goals/projects only when we are not busy, or when everything else is done, or when we have spare time, the likelihood that we will achieve those goals is relatively small. Most of us find ourselves in situations where we have more things to do than we have time for. No matter how many things get crossed off our To Do lists there is always a backlog of things that remain to be done.

Time must be <u>made</u> for long-term projects that are important, no matter what our present circumstances.

The only practical way forward in this situation is to consciously take the decision to make time, on a regular basis, for things that are important to us and to our long-term future and happiness. The operative words here are "make time". The time we need to accomplish long-term projects is not going to magically manifest itself to us. We have to make room for important and strategic things no matter how "busy" we are, or what our personal situation is. This sometimes means that some less important things don't get done. But, no matter how much time we had, there would always be more things that we could do, or that we think we should do. Given that this is the way things are, we should not feel guilty taking time for the important things.

The alternative, of letting busyness or business create a barrier that stops us from making progress on long-term goals, should not be an option. All busyness does is rob us of accomplishments that would give us long-lasting pleasure and satisfaction. There is absolutely no virtue in being busy. We are wasting our time and putting our quality of life in jeopardy if we succumb to busyness. We are far better off investing time in things that will improve the quality of our life and hopefully contribute to making the world a better place.

Law 5: Invest time in personal growth

There is an old Chinese proverb which says: when you stop learning, whether at eighty or twenty, you are old! We do not grow unless we take action by mastering new skills, accepting a new challenge, reading new things, writing and, most importantly, thinking deeply, intensively and creatively about new problems and issues. Learning, is to people, what water is to plants. Without learning, we lose our vitality and our zest for living.

A part of your time is yours to invest in your own development and growth no matter what your current circumstances are.

Unless we are consistently investing at least some of our time in learning and growing we are failing to use our time wisely -our life will lack balance and be pointed in the direction of shallow living and stagnation.

A passing comment on reading, I came across recently, sums up the situation: a person who does not read is no better off than a person who cannot read. This indictment may be applied with equal force to other forms of learning and thinking. Through learning, and nothing else, we learn how to live. For what can life be, but a journey of learning.

Law 6: Invest time in other people

It was Benjamin Franklin who said the noblest question we can ask is: *what good can we do in the world?* A preoccupation with satisfying only our own needs is unlikely to give us, or others, much long-term happiness. Nor is such a focus likely to contribute significantly to making the world a better place.

The greatest gift we can give another human being is our time and our undivided attention.

Giving time to others can be one of the most satisfying things that any human being can do. In these times, when everyone is so "busy" and preoccupied with their own affairs there is not that much sharing of time between couples, between parents and children, between friends, between neighbours and between people in general. No one has much "quality" time to spend and share with others. Most of us need this quality time with others to share our experiences, to have fun, to work through our and their problems, to get the feeling that we and they are important, that there is someone who cares about us, and about what we do and what we think. By sharing experiences with others we increase the quality of those experiences. It is not the same thing, to have climbed the highest mountain all by yourself, as sharing the climb and the experience with someone else. Sharing time with others can also stimulate our and their personal growth and learning. The consequences of not sharing time with others is that we usually become more selfish, less caring and more unhappy and frustrated.

In sharing time with others we should seek to make that time creative and constructive. It should be used to, where we can, create opportunities and possibilities for others and to make them happy or feel special or important. A day should not pass where we fail to do at least one little thing that makes someone else feel happy or special. At the same time, spending time with others should not be devoted to imposing our values upon them or inflating our ego. Such time is wasted, as is time spent gossiping, politicking and criticizing people behind their backs. More often than not, when we are with others, it is far better just to listen and to try to see things from their perspective, and their circumstances, rather than from our own -the latter might be quite different. Some people use a lot of their time with others doing things for them. While in some cases this is appropriate, it is far better, in proverbial terms, to teach people how to fish than to keep giving them fish.

More than anything else, in the time we spend with others, we should be looking to set an example in what we do and in the way we do things. What we do by example is far more likely to have a positive impact on others than anything we might say to them.

Giving freely of our time to other people, and doing things for others without being prompted or asked, is something that adds a little extra to our lives. Such deeds, whether we are on the giving or the receiving end, are uplifting experiences that can influence our and their future behaviour. One of these incidents happened to me recently when I travelled overseas. Before I went, I had cleared out a lot of junk from under our house and put it in a large container that I had hired. The container was located outside our backyard in the local park. When the guy came to cart away the container (while I was away) he decided that I had piled in too much rubbish. He "solved" his problem by simply dumping a big pile of the rubbish in the park. The local park ranger promptly turned up and told my wife that she had to move the rubbish forthwith or we would have to pay a hefty fine. My wife's welcoming words, when I arrived home, after a twenty-six hour flight, were that I would need to immediately set about removing the rubbish. Reluctantly, I got changed and headed out the back gate to see what needed to be done. When I got there, to my complete surprise, the rubbish was all gone. Our next-door neighbours who had witnessed the whole drama, without even a word to my wife, had taken the load of junk off to the local dump. When this happened, I felt guilty because I knew just how busy my neighbours were, but, at the same time, I felt how lucky we were to live where we do.

Some people spend time with others, and doing things for others but their efforts are restricted to a small circle of close friends and relatives. If we are to play our part to make the world a better place we must be prepared also, at times, to give time to others outside our usual sphere of existence.

This kind of selfless giving of time to people who we may never see again is a vital ingredient to making the world a better place for us all. Several years ago my family and I went off to live in Scotland for a year. I vividly remember, on the second day we were there, going up to an old lady and asking her directions to some particular place. To my surprise, the old lady, recognizing that I was a foreigner, insisted on taking me by the arm and guiding me the 200 meters or so to my destination -after that I felt very much at home in Scotland. This incident may be contrasted to another incident that happened to me in my travels. This time I went up to a man selling papers and asked for some information. His response was: "did I think he was paid to give information to people" -you can imagine how welcome I felt in that place.

There are some people who feel there is little that they, personally, can do to make the world a better place. It is relatively easy to show that this assumption is probably wrong. Of course, what we do, does not reach everybody directly but its effect can still be far-reaching. The human race is far more connected than most people imagine. A little mathematics can help show this. Let us assume you know and interact directly with 100 people (for most people this number would be a very conservative estimate). Also suppose that each of these 100 people knows and directly interacts with 100 other people (i.e., excluding the ones you know). What this tells us, using the "I know someone who knows someone" principle, is that their is a person-distance of only one between you and 10,000 people (100x100). Taking the argument just one step further, there is a person distance of only two between you and 1,000,000 people. It is well within the realms of possibility that, by your actions, you can have an impact on people that are separated from you by a small person-distance. Of course, no claim is made that this model is an accurate representation of reality. However, the principle that it embodies, suggests that what each of us does can make a difference.

Law 7: Focus on the vital few (Pareto Principle)

Some of the books that have been written about time focus upon how to get more done in less time. While this is laudable, it should be tempered by making sure that what we are doing is important and relevant to our overall goals and objectives. Using time effectively is not simply about doing more, it is about doing what is important and strategic. A useful device that can help us in this regard is the Pareto Principle cited below.

Beware, 20% of the time invested can yield 80% of the returns obtained, while 80% of the time invested may yield only the remaining 20% of returns

What the Pareto Principle responds to is that, in whatever the situation, not all things are equally important for achieving a desired outcome. That is, there are usually many variables associated with any problem, situation, process or goal that we want to achieve. However, in a lot of cases, as few as 20% of these variables will playa major role in achieving the desired outcome. In other words, for any situation, the variables have an "importance distribution". We need to understand this.

The Pareto Principle is important for several reasons. For one thing, it seems to apply in such a wide range of circumstances. In what ever we are doing we should therefore ask: is the Pareto Principle relevant in this situation? It urges us to model and abstract about the situation we are dealing with. It suggests a way of simplifying things and of focussing only on the most important things that are likely to give us the highest return for our effort. This principle is also vitally important for prioritizing and for developing strategies for improvement.

In seeking to apply the Pareto Principle it is important to use measurement, logic, commonsense, observation and whatever other rigorous tools we can bring to bear to decide what are the most important variables or factors that we need to focus on to achieve our objectives.

Law 8: The last 20% makes the difference

The Pareto Principle tells us that it is wise to concentrate our effort on the important things. This is a reasonable strategy, but there are also a lot of situations where what seems to operate is what we will call the Anti-Pareto principle.

Between good and the best is a large effort

Situations are numerous where a 20% effort will return you 80% of what it is possible to achieve but where you will need to invest another four times that effort to be the best or to make an outstanding achievement.

It is easiest to convey this principle by way of examples. Take the case of swimming or running. It would be possible, with a little effort, for many people to clock times for given distances that were only 20% slower than the times clocked by world record holders. However, you would most likely find that athletes in the world record-holder league probably invest at least four times more effort and time to achieve the results that they achieve. It is a similar situation with study, if you focus only on the important things, you may be able to achieve a result of 80%. However to get the extra 20% that would give you a perfect result of 100% it is likely that a lot more effort would be required (maybe up to four times the effort that got you the 80% result).

There are many situations where, in seeking to achieve worthy long-term goals, we want to do something that is outstanding compared to what others achieve. If this is the case, then we must be prepared to have to live by the Anti-Pareto Principle. Outstanding achievement never comes cheaply in terms of the investment of time required. Famous Olympic sprinter Carl Lewis summed it up when he said: if you want to be the best you have to work the hardest. At the same time, simply investing a large amount of time is not enough to guarantee an outstanding achievement. *We must be prepared to work smart as well as hard.* Sporting achievements of today, compared with those in the past, bear witness to the advantage of using both the Pareto and Anti-Pareto Principles.

The important lesson to learn from both the Pareto and Anti-Pareto Principles is that we must assess any given situation to see which, or what mix of the two principles is likely to apply before deciding how much time we need to invest to achieve the outcomes we desire.

Law 9: Worthy results take time

Most things worth achieving, by their very nature, involve substantial investments of time and effort. It is the time and effort it takes to achieve something, which gives it, its' value.

Time slips away from those who expect results from their investment too quickly

To expect a quick return for any time investment in a worthy project is an unrealistic expectation. If we expect quick results, or rapid progress, we are likely to be disappointed and risk being tempted not to see the project through. What is worse, if we quit a worthwhile project we waste our initial effort and the time invested. We also undermine our confidence to tackle and complete other worthwhile projects. If we do this too often, we will reach a state where we no longer try to tackle large projects.

There is no great harm in impatience, provided it IS channelled at reaffirming our commitment to a project.

Law 10: Avoid useless activity

There are many things that each and everyone of us does that will not give either ourselves, or anyone else, pleasure or satisfaction, nor will they make the world a better place. If we want to be more effective users of time we must mount an on-going campaign to identify and eliminate such habits, behaviours and activities. In doing this we must be careful about what we classify as useless.

Never invest time in useless activity

There are two kinds of useless or unnecessary activity. Doing something that is not worth doing and using a clumsy or inefficient way to do something that needs to be done.

The Pareto Principle can offer some guidance with regard to useless activity. In doing things it is important to concentrate on the main game rather than put a lot of effort into peripheral issues. This is where perfectionists sometimes come unstuck. We should invest time on peripheral issues only in proportion to their importance. It is, for instance, not worthwhile putting all your effort into cleaning the windscreen of your car when the brakes need fixing.

Law 11: Do not dwell on achievement, the past or failure

A strong emphasis throughout this book is upon achieving substantive long-term goals. This emphasis should not however be taken as a cue for overvaluing our achievements. There are three key negative consequences that can flow from overvaluing our past achievements and the whole notion of achievement.

They are:

- we indulge in self-important and self-centred behaviour that most other people perceive as boring, irritating, belittling or even pathetic
- we stop growing, developing and taking up new opportunities and therefore fail to realize our full potential, or
- we become obsessive about achieving more and more goals at the expense of our quality of life.

It is far wiser to see achievement, not so much as an end in itself, but rather, for the quality of the experience it gives us along the way. A prime example where we see the negative consequences of failing to do this is in today's university education. Past generations of students attended university for the quality of the experience, whereas today, many of the students are there for the piece of paper. As a consequence, the whole atmosphere, quality of learning, and scope for personal growth, has changed. This criticism is not intended to be a direct indictment of today's students but rather it is a criticism of the way social attitudes have changed as the world has become more materially-minded and competition for jobs has grown.

Chapter 3:
Laws of time utilization

Everything has been thought of before, the problem is to think of it again -- Goethe

Making effective use of our time

How we utilize our time ultimately governs the amount we have to devote to long-term goals and what we are able to achieve. In our use of time we need to put into practice the strategic principles of time investment. To maximize the impact of these principles a second set is needed -the laws of time utilization.

The key to utilizing our time effectively is to always consciously place a high value on our time each and every day. Doing this helps us to ward off distractions, prioritize, keep focussed and to use an effective process for investing time. The rest is then relatively easy.

We will now spell out a set of laws of time utilization and provide a brief commentary on each.

Law 1: Value your time

Most of us do not consistently place a high enough value on our time. This is the single greatest impediment to our effective use of time. Without conscious, consistent and actively planned and prioritized effort, we are unlikely to place a high value on how we spend our time each day, each week, each year and each decade.

Those who value their time have sown the seeds to acquire gold

People fail to value their time because they do not see or treat it as their most precious resource. Only by placing a high value on our time are we likely to accomplish even one, let alone many long-term goals that will give us long-lasting pleasure and satisfaction -the gold we seek.

To place a very high value on our time we need to passionately adopt and live by this policy:

That from now onwards, each and every day, we will value our use of time.

Learning, and consistently living by this value, alone, will get us at least half the way to effectively using our time. There are many things we can do to value our time but three things are pivotal: having clear goals, prioritizing so that the most important things regularly get their portion of time and planning both on a daily basis and for the longer term.

Law 2: Let the goal be the guide

In whatever we do, if we want to use our time effectively, we should at all times keep in mind what our priority goal or goals are.

Begin with the end in mind, continue with the end in mind, and finish with the end in mind.

By a goal, we do not mean some vague idea that floats around among our thoughts from time to time. Goals that can help us use our time effectively must be very clear. At the very least, they must be written down in the clearest possible terms. As part of writing down a goal we should specify a realistic time when we want to, and by when are really committed to achieving it. We should also have a clear understanding of why the goal is so important to us, why we are committed to achieving it, and what the benefits are that will flow from achieving it. We should also list what not achieving the goal will cost us. In some cases we may use visualization or any other device that motivates us to make our goals more real.

Goals need the sort potency we have described to be able to create momentum, maintain our staying power and guarantee we will follow through until they are fully realized. When our goals are potent we can remain focussed, measure our progress, ward off distractions, overcome setbacks and motivate ourselves to consistently stick to our priorities on a daily, weekly, monthly and yearly basis - whatever it takes.

Clearly a strong goal-focus is crucial to investing our time wisely. There are however two things that we need to be mindful of in employing a strong goal-oriented approach. First, we should be sure we are shooting for the right goal. When we start out to achieve a long-term goal our understanding of what we really want may change as our understanding evolves along the way. Therefore we must not be completely rigid about our original goals. Other possibilities or opportunities may arise that offer a better outcome. In these cases, if there are clear benefits in altering a goal, and provided we have carefully weighed up the situation, then we should be prepared to change. We should be strongly focussed on our goals but, at the same time, we should be flexible enough to make changes if they are needed.

The critical thing about using goals is not to fall into the trap of attempting to achieve more than a small number of major long-term goals at anyone time. Each additional goal, beyond about two, starts to dilute our effort and erode our effective use of time. I learned this lesson the hard way several years ago when I started to focus on making better use of my time. As I got better at using my time I took on more projects. After I had done this for several months it became clear that I was not making the progress I had hoped for with any of them. Now that I have switched to concentrating on only a smaller number of long-term goals in parallel (at most three) I have been much happier with my rate of progress. The same situation applies on a daily basis. Your effort will be much more effective if you only concentrate on two or three major tasks in a day. It is alright to work on a whole bunch of To Do's, but only after the work on the long-term projects is done. I used to carry home a large briefcase full of things to do at night. Now, at best, I carry home a small folder.

Law 3: Prioritize your use of time

Having made the decision to value our time and focus on achieving our long-term goals we can start to develop the habits that will allow us to do three things: identify which of our goals have the highest priority, invest our time accordingly to achieve these goals and ensure that we stick to these priorities. Making these things a reality is not something that will just happen overnight. We have to keep practising and practising setting our priorities, rejecting things that stop us from sticking to our plans and reassessing each day and each week whether or not we are living the value of valuing our time. If we are not, we need to keep monitoring and changing our behaviour until we consistently value our time.

Those who value their time, and prioritize its use, are nurturing the plant that will yield them gold

Usually we do not regard something as a precious resource unless:

- we know there is not much of it left, or
- there is more, that is important to us, that we want to use a resource for, than there is resource available.

Use time or it will use you

If for example, we knew this was our last day alive we would probably place a much greater value on how we spent our time. Instead of going about our business as usual, we would think very carefully about what we did, how we did it, and how much time we were prepared to spend on each activity. While this is an extreme situation it can serve to make us question two things: what is important to us, and whether we should spend a significant amount of time doing things that are most important to us. Clearly, if we don't, we are not being true to ourselves and we are sowing the seeds for unhappy times ahead.

Often, before we can do things that are most important to us we need to accomplish other things. These other things then have to become the most important things we can do now in order to accomplish what we want to accomplish in the longer term. There are always things that are most important that we can do NOW, and in the immediate future, which are a step towards what we want to achieve in the longer term.

Really coming to terms with this is a very important first step to placing a much higher value on our time. It allows us to ask questions like: if I spend time doing this will it contribute to what I want accomplish in the longer term. In other words, it allows us • to start prioritizing what we do now in order to accomplish what we want achieve in the longer term. This should always be an important guiding principle that we employ to decide what is important to do NOW and what is important to do NEXT.

We place a much higher value on our time when we have important long-term things that we are passionate about doing and we know those things are going to require a large investment of effort and time to accomplish.

Law 4: Plan your time

Planning the use of our time plays a vital role in helping us to manage our priorities and achieve our long-term goals. Plans are the key facilitating mechanism that enable us not only to place a high value on our time, and to prioritise, but also to assist us to invest wisely the limited time we have.

Time slips away from those who fail to plan how they will use it

What we must recognize is that time always passes and that there are always things than we can do that occupy our time. However, without a

clear plan, it is unlikely that we will use our time effectively to achieve long-term goals. A plan gives us focus. It causes us to change our behaviour and it allows us to measure our progress. A plan also makes it easier for us to set and maintain our priorities in the face of disruptions and distractions. Proceeding without a plan is like going sailing without a rudder.

There are a variety of ways we can specify plans. If plans are to be effective they need to be specified over a number of different time periods -a day, a week, a month, a year, or even a five or ten year period. What we do each day, each week and each month should be contributing to what we want to accomplish over a year, over two years or over a five or a ten year period. A plan should always be written down. As someone once said: until you commit your goals and plans to paper you have seeds without soil. A plan should consist of a clear description of what you want to accomplish in a specified time period. It is not enough to say what you want to achieve -you must also say when you commit to achieving it.

Planning needs to be done consistently every day. Investment of time in our long-term goals should always be given highest priority on a daily, weekly and monthly basis. The following strategy works well. At the end of each day, we should plan how we intend to spend the next day. In this planning we must be sure to fit in the time to be invested in our long-term goals. The strategy I use is to spend time on my long-term goals very early in the day, when I am fresh, and before the distractions and disruptions have any chance to interfere. Remember, it is small steps taken consistently, on a daily basis, day in and day out, which, in the end, enable us to achieve our long-term goals.

In a similar way, at the end of each week, we should layout our plans for the next week. The goals we set for a week should be used to guide our planning, scheduling and prioritization on a daily basis. Monthly, half yearly and yearly planning processes should be used in a similar way, although the latter have a much more strategic focus.

It is not enough just to prioritize and plan. What we must do is follow through and execute our plans. Our commitment to our long-term goals should be non-negotiable. We must however, sometimes be prepared to revise and readjust our plans in the light of progress and/or circumstances. These adjustments should not be at the expense of regularly making progress with our long-term goals. If things happen that upset our commitments to our long-term goals on a short-term basis then we should be prepared to take other action and make other sacrifices to make up for time lost. If there is real commitment to long-term goals then occasions should be rare where they are not given their due. Other tasks of lesser priority may suffer but our commitment to our long-term goals should hold fast.

Before breaking off our discussion on planning it is important to raise the issue of peoples' attitude to planning. Most people have a strong resistance to planning even though, at least intellectually, they know that it is a good idea to plan. Why is this so? There would seem to be at least two main reasons why people avoid or neglect to plan: some people naively see planning as a waste of time -they feel it is better to spend the time actually doing something. Others feel that having a plan, which they have to follow, takes away their freedom and their spontaneity. There is some truth in both these responses. However, the benefits of having plans and sticking to them by far outweigh their disadvantages. In fact, those who have a plan and follow through usually derive considerable pleasure from doing so. It is only by using plans consistently, for a substantial period of time, that we come to realize their importance in achieving long-term goals.

Law 5: Stick to your priorities and plans

It is all very well to have grand plans and priorities for the use of our time. What really counts is whether we stick to those plans and priorities. It sounds straightforward to draw up a plan for our use of time on a daily and weekly basis, etc and then to follow that plan. However, particularly when we are starting off, there is usually a large gap between having a plan and being able to follow it through. There are always other things that come up which provide perfectly good reasons for abandoning our commitments to our plan.

Gold cometh in plenty to those who consistently value their time, consistently prioritize its use wisely, and consistently stick to their priorities

We should expect that it will take a concerted effort, over a considerable period of time, with a number of false starts and frustrations, before we start to come close to rigorously and consistently sticking to our priorities. The important thing is not to get discouraged by our initial failures and poor attempts. Learning to stick to priorities is a skill that can only be developed to a high level by a lot of practice, persistence and patience. It is important to recognize that to develop the habit of sticking to our priorities most of us need to make some fundamental changes in our behaviour. A technique is suggested in the next chapter for developing good habits and curing bad habits. Once we master this skill we will start to have access to the time we need to accomplish our long-term goals.

Law 6: Guard your time

Having made the decision to value our time and to invest it doing things that are most important to us does not guarantee we will spend our time doing those things. Consider the following exercise: watch what happens when you plan how you are going to spend your time for a day. At the end of the day, check whether or not you achieved the things you set out to achieve. If you are like most people you will not have accomplished anywhere near what you originally planned.

There are always external influences and habits which, if we let them, erode our efforts to value our time and invest it doing what is important to us now.

Time slips away from those who do not guard its use

If, having made the commitment to invest time to achieve important long-term goals, we then do not avoid interruptions, much of our effort will be wasted.

To make the job of guarding our time easier we must do three things:

- make it clear to those around us that there are regular critical times when we are committed to doing things and that we do not want this schedule to be interrupted by anyone for any reason, save fire, flood or famine,

- we must also choose or create an environment that enables us to minimize the risk of disruptions when we are working on our long-term goals,

- finally, we need to ensure that every time we invest time to achieve our long-term goals, we get the most out of that investment.

If we develop the habits and the discipline that allow us to operate in this way, we will not be an easy prey for disruptions and distractions. Of course, there will be times when other things interfere in our commitments to our long-term goals. However, if we have developed strong and consistent habits for guarding and using our time, occasional exceptions and deviations will not significantly slow our momentum. For a long time I have maintained the habit of running three times a week. Sometimes I travel and miss my schedule. However, because the habit is so well established, as soon as I return, I fall back into my running routine without any trouble. To develop a useful sustainable habit for most people takes it least one or two months.

Law 7: Measure your use of time

At first sight, suggesting that we should measure how long we spend doing important things might seem like a bit of bureaucracy that is peripheral to getting the main task done. While it takes a little extra time to measure critical time spent, the return on the investment of that time, far outweighs its cost.

It is well known (the Hawthorn Effect) that measuring some aspect of our behaviour causes us to change that behaviour. What measurement does is provide feedback. Feedback, in turn, is information that we can use for three purposes:

- to measure progress
- to identify problems
- to guide changes in our behavior to make us more effective in our use of time

Those who measure their strategic use of time, improve their effectiveness.

Exactly what we measure is vital. Given that measurement influences behaviour, then if we measure the wrong things, we may not get the outcomes or the improvements we want. Take the case of the software company who told its programmers it was going to measure how many lines of program they produced each month. Guess what happened? The programmers all started producing more lines of program per month. This did not mean that the quality of their programs improved, or that they finished the jobs they had to do quicker. All it meant was that they changed their behaviour so that bigger programs were written in a given time period. If you measure "monkey behaviour" in people, you will reinforce monkey behaviour. What we can learn from this is that the things we measure influence what we focus upon. Put another way, there is a compelling tendency for that which gets measured to get done. Measurement can therefore be used as a powerful instrument of change. It impartially provides either positive (encouragement) or negative feedback (that is, it signals the need for change). The

Use time or it will use you

importance of feedback is that it allows us to monitor and control the direction of change.

We must therefore think very carefully about what we choose to measure. If we make the right choices, we can bring about the sort of changes and improvements that we want.

To avoid wasting time on measurement we should apply the Pareto Principle. It tells us that, of all the things we could measure, only 20% of them will return 80% of the value of doing the measurements.

The most obvious and critical thing for us to measure is *"uninterrupted time spent working on our long-term goals"* -this is quality time invested. Of course, all measurement should be preceded by planning -we need to plan how we will invest our time to achieve our strategic long-term goals then measure our effectiveness, analyse the results, analyse our behaviour, and make the changes that are necessary.

Before leaving the discussion of measurement it is worth exploring the consequences of not measuring how we use our time. Our claim is that it would be highly unlikely that we would achieve anywhere near the same level of improvement in our use of time. Failing to measure, is like trying to get better at hitting the bulls-eye in a shooting gallery that is in complete darkness. If you did this day after day it is unlikely that you would ever get any better. No feedback, no improvement! As a second example, imagine two warring galleons. Do you think they would increase their chances of hitting one another if they could not see where their cannon balls were landing in the water relative to the enemy -I doubt it. Without feedback you have no accurate measure, either of what you are achieving or of what you need to do to improve. Furthermore you lose the psychological impact of measurement on behaviour. We are not machines, but that does not mean we can't use measurement to our advantage to improve our effective use of time to achieve strategic goals. While it is okay to apply measurement to ourselves we should be very wary about applying it to other people!

Law 8: Use an effective process

There is almost always more than one way to do anything we care to think about. And, these different ways of doing things, are not all equally efficient.

The process used determines the quality of the outcome and the time expended

An effective process is one that, relative to other alternatives, uses time more economically and produces a quality outcome. It also eliminates defects and minimizes the amount of rework necessary.

There are usually too many tasks that we perform to have time to worry about optimizing them all. Instead we should let the Pareto Principle be our guide in choosing what to optimize. Remember 80% of the gains are likely to come from 20% of the tasks we perform. Prime candidates for improvement are those processes that involve lengthy amounts of time and those we perform frequently. When it comes to optimizing a particular process the Pareto Principle again comes into effect. Rather than focus on optimizing all aspects of the process, we should instead, focus on optimizing the critical parts of the process that will give the greatest returns for our efforts.

To make processes more effective there are a number of things take into account. Included are the following questions and comments:

- are the preconditions (that is, the conditions that apply before we start) for activating the process precisely and completely specified.
- can we make the processes simpler
- can the process be broken up into simpler disjoint sub tasks that can be performed independently and thereby avoid the cost of task switching
- can the order of steps in the process be changed to make the process more effective
- are all the things that we do in the process absolutely necessary
- do the separate sub-tasks compose efficiently
- is there a completely different way of tackling the problem that would be better.

As a general rule, when we wish to assess and improve the effectiveness of a process, we need to have available the best possible information. Both quantitative and qualitative information should be sought about a process. This suggests the need to measure and track key variables or parameters and to assess how we or others that use a process "feel" about it. These measurements and qualitative input can be used to guide and assess improvements in effectiveness.

With processes, we should always be vigilant and looking for ways to improve their effectiveness in the interests of utilizing our time more effectively.

Law 9: Avoid Frequent Task-Switching

Many people frequently switch from doing one thing, to doing something else -we call this behaviour task-switching. That something else, may be totally unrelated, or it may be a disjoint task that contributes to the same overall objective, or it may be a task that has some overlap with the current task. In most instances, task-switching has a significant negative impact on our overall efficiency. When we exhibit this behaviour it usually means we are lacking in focus.

It takes less time to do N disjoint tasks separately, one at a time, from start to end, than to switch between them

In my own case, looking back on the way I used to work, I now realize that, for a long time, I was a chronic task-switcher. I would sit at my desk and look at the large pile of things I had to do. I would start on one thing for a few minutes then something else on my desk would catch my eye or pop into my mind and I would switch to doing that because it was urgent. Then there would a knock at the door, or the phone would ring, and I would be off on another tangent. This whole way of working would go on day after day without anything satisfying being accomplished. There is no need for most people to function like that. Unfortunately many people seem to let things happen this way.

There are a number of common causes of task-switching: we don't have a clear idea of what we are trying to achieve, we are uncertain what to do next, we do not have a clearly defined process or we are distracted by something else.

Task-switching cuts down our effectiveness. When we switch from one task to another our concentration is broken. And if, prior to the switch, we have been working in a state-of-flow (i.e., at our full capacity) then, in the switch to the new activity, there will be a period of low productivity until we build up again to a state-of-flow. The higher the frequency at which we switch between tasks the less effective we become. There is also one other important negative aspect of frequently switching between tasks -it impacts the quality of the work we do. This is because our concentration level is not as high as if we were focussed and working in a concentrated state-of-flow.

It might be argued there are times when task-switching makes a lot of sense. Consider, for example, that you are working away on something when, all of a sudden, you get a good idea about something else. Obviously, we cannot stop such random thoughts from happening. So what should you do when they happen. My advice is simple. If the idea is something important that you want to follow up on later, then the best thing is to keep a note-pad and pencil within reach -then you can quickly jot down the idea and get straight back to what you were working on. If you don't do this, you are likely to start worrying that you will not remember later what you had thought of that needed attending to. This too, can erode your attention while working on the current task. When I am working on my computer I keep the electronic note-pad opened up so that I can quickly jot down ideas. Earlier on, when I got an idea I used to take the extra trouble to record the idea in that part of my file system where it belonged. This used to cause a major disruption to my flow. I also have a note-pad beside my computer which I use to jot down ideas.

The only time that task-switching can be justified is when there is genuine overlap between tasks. This happens if we get a less efficient outcome from doing first one task and, when that is completed, the second task. In making films, task-switching is frequently used and can be easily justified. All the scenes in a given location are usually shot at the same time rather than in the order in which they appear in the edited movie. This saves on setup costs.

We have already given a number of reasons why task-switching is inefficient. There is also the other side of the story. When we don't switch we are in effect separating our concerns. In other words, we are concentrating our effort on a simpler process. The advantage of this is that working on a simpler task is more efficient and, at the same time, less error prone.

An important message that flows from all this discussion is that we need to analyse tasks that we do to see whether they can be broken down into disjoint sub-tasks that could be done more efficiently, separately. Quite often we find that people are not even aware that what they are doing involves task-switching. Take for example, the task of writing. Many people jumble together the tasks of planning, writing, editing, restructuring, polishing, correcting and proof-reading. They view the task of writing as a single process involving all these activities. This view of writing is completely flawed. People who write this way waste a lot of time. The biggest mistake in writing is to start writing without a plan and then have to plan and restructure as you go. This habit is probably the one that has the greatest impact on reducing a writer's effectiveness.

The following illustrates the process I use to do my writing. When I am writing a particular chapter or section or article the first thing I do is write down the heading and attach to it a little device called a planning pad. The planning pad I used to plan and guide the writing of this section is shown below. It consists of a table of two columns, a narrow one in which I can insert numbers and a second one in which I can insert brief descriptions (one to two lines) of major points I want to write about.

	PLANNING PAD
1	what is task switching - TS is a behaviour
1b	the tasks may contribute to whole but be disjoint
1c	why we task switch - lack of clearly defined process or lack of clear goals are uncertain what to do next, we are distracted = how do we stop it
2	why is task switching bad
3	effects of task switching
3a	task-switching breaks concentration
3b	task-switching interrupts flow
3c	each time start new task is startup cost
3d	task-switching makes less focussed erodes quality
3e	task-switching means you are not focussed
4a	when is task switching justified
4b	only time switch if costs more
4c	we can't stop random thoughts that need attention
4d	if something else bothering you write to notepad
4e	use a physical or electronic notepad on desk
S	separation on concerns simplifies process
Sa	benefits of not task switching
Sb	simpler processes gen more effic and less errors
6a	need to analyze to see if is sub-task disjoint
6b	example - writing, editing, restructuring, proof

To do my planning for a section, I simply write down points that come to me in random order. To stimulate my thinking I ask questions based on what, why, when, where, how, and who. When I have run out of ideas I then go through the list of points with the intent of ordering and grouping them in a way that best expresses how I want to arrange the ideas in the particular section. I can do this efficiently, simply by putting numbers in the first column. Sometimes I add alphabetic extensions to the numbers to fine tune where they need to be grouped to fit in. I then use the SORT function on my computer to order the rows according to the numbering scheme I have used. After this I take another look at the order I have made and make any adjustments by altering the point numbers. I then sort again. This gives a good plan for writing a section. Usually I will plan a section sometime before I choose to write it. This gives me the chance to mull it over a little in the background and to think up new points. Since I have been writing in this way, I have found a marked improvement in my efficiency, and in the clarity of the structure of what I write.

The second major mistake that a lot of people make when writing is to worry about editing, restructuring and polishing as they go. These are quite separate tasks to that of creative writing. If we do these tasks as we write, we are continually interrupting the flow of writing and shifting our concentration. This slows us down considerably. Such tasks are better done after, separately. We can then devote our full attention to them, and do a much better job, more efficiently.

My overall assessment is that writing in this way is much more efficient, and more enjoyable. And, as a bonus, the outcome needs much less editing and restructuring What is more, I am usually much happier with the quality of the final outcome. The other advantage is that I find it much easier to get into a state-of-flow writing this way.

Law 10: Don't just twiddle your thumbs at road-blocks

Road-blocks can be deadly time-wasters. By a road-block, I mean something that stops our flow and stops us from getting on with the task we are currently working on;

When you see a road-block, don't just sit there, take quick and decisive action.

This law is a complement of the task-switching law. It is also related to effective task composition. What I am suggesting is that switching tasks is a very good idea when the only alternative is to just stall and not do anything effective while we are waiting. We need to be always prepared to switch tasks when a hold-up occurs in the task we are currently working on. This often requires some forward planning. The following very simple domestic example illustrates the principle. When I go shopping, or to pick up my daughter from fencing, etc, I always take one of my scientific journals to read. This way, if I have to wait, I get something useful done rather than end up just sitting around and getting frustrated.

Road-blocks come in all shapes and forms. They have two fundamental causes. Either we are in a situation where we are waiting on someone else to do something, or we do not have direct access to something that is vital to progressing the current task. Before switching to an alternative it is usually a good strategy to take some action that will expedite the situation and resolve the hold-up.

Anticipating, and having an alternative productive task to do when a roadblock occurs, is an excellent habit to cultivate. Also, recognizing that what we are facing is in fact a roadblock, is important. Not all road-blocks are obvious. Sometimes we can dither around with a problem and waste time because we have not recognized, or we have ignored, that what we are confronting is indeed a road-block.

Law 11: Expend the time required

The advice: a goal without a deadline is not a goal at all is often given. There is a very good reason for setting deadlines for things -they tend to change our behaviour and to give us greater focus and motivation to meet the deadline. However, there is a negative side to setting deadlines, if the ones we set, are unrealistic. A deadline is only useful if it helps us to use our time more effectively. A deadline, is therefore a double-edged sword -something that, if used properly, will help us, and, if abused, will work against us.

Time slips away from those who try to accomplish a goal in too short a time

People set unrealistic deadlines for achieving goals for one of three reasons:

- either they are not fully committed to successfully achieving the goal, or
- they are inexperienced at estimating their own efficiency, or

- they want what the long-term goal can give them, but they are unwilling to pay the price it will cost to achieve.

Without exception, worthwhile long-term goals never come cheap.

There are a number of consequences that flow from not taking deadline setting seriously and from not setting realistic deadlines. In the first instance, if we don't take deadlines seriously, we cannot expect them to work for us in a positive way. Unrealistic deadlines do not motivate us to be more productive. Instead, they undermine our efforts by destroying our credibility with ourselves and others. They may also force us to sacrifice quality and end up having to do a lot of rework later. Unrealistic deadlines create frustration and lead to overwork. Both of these things, slow us down. People only work at their full potential when they are enjoying what they are doing. There are absolutely no benefits to be had from applying unrealistic time pressures. This is in no way meant to imply that we cannot, or should not, try to achieve remarkable feats in a short amount of time. Such feats are possible if we have the motivation and focus, the right conditions, we enjoy what we are doing and we are not hurting or depriving others.

As a general rule, we should set deadlines that put enough pressure on us so that only by working consistently and effectively over a sustained period, will we be able to realize our goal. Deadlines should not completely distort the way we live and force us to sacrifice other things that are important to us -particularly, our enjoyment for what we are

Use time or it will use you

doing, our health, our relationships, our commitments and the other things that significantly affect our quality of life.

In setting deadlines for achieving long-term goals we should therefore base our estimates on what we know we are capable of when working consistently at our full potential. In saying this, we should definitely not be limited by our past achievements. If we are continually becoming more effective then these estimates will be too long. As we proceed, we should also reassess and readjust our deadlines. The important thing is to always have a realistic estimate of how much longer it is going to take to realize a goal. The further along we get, the more accurate should be our estimate of the completion time.

When we are faced with a personal situation that involves an unrealistic deadline that must be met we have only two options: change the scope of what must be achieved or try to find a way to radically improve our effectiveness by finding a more creative way of realizing our goal.

Law 12: Accomplish all you can

It is not enough just to invest time in our long-term goals if we want to use our time effectively. Consider, for example, the following two scenarios:

"I am going to work on my long-term goal for XX hours this day/week/month"

"I am going to accomplish YY in the XX hours I invest in my long-term goal this day/week/month"

Which of the two strategies do you think is likely to lead to the more effective use of time in a given period?

There are plenty of people who commit to investing time to achieve long-term goals but make the mistake of not setting targets for what they want to accomplish in every period of time they invest. It does not matter what your long-term goal is -whether you plan to win an Olympic Gold medal, build a yacht, or write a book, there should be an objective or a goal associated with every slot of time you invest. It is like setting sail from North America to Australia by heading in the general direction but without bothering to set a course for the journey. Achieving long-term goals is very much like sailing over great oceans -we must have our course set at all times, and be constantly monitoring to see that we have not been blown off course.

The point of this whole discussion is to suggest that we should always associate goals with short and long periods of time that we invest. If we don't have goals for each period of time we invest, then it is highly likely we will not accomplish as much as if we had set a goal to be achieved in that time period. A goal to be accomplished, in a given time period, gives us motivation and focus -both are important factors for using time effectively. Goals also allow us to monitor progress and adjust our strategies.

Time slips away from the person who tries to accomplish too little in a given period of time

In order to make extensive use of goal-setting to improve our effective use of time, it is important that the goals we set, match as accurately as possible, what we are capable of accomplishing in a given time period. It is therefore important, through consistent observation and measurement, for each of us to evolve a clear picture of our capability so that we can set better short-term goals that are just within our reach.

Law 13: Invest at the right time

If we look at champion golfers, or batsmen playing cricket, we will notice how important timing is. In contrast, an amateur might appear to exert a much greater effort but achieve results that are no where near as impressive. So clearly, the return we get is not directly proportional to the effort we apply. A similar situation applies with time. There is an appropriate time to do things if we want to get the maximum return on our investment of time.

To gain maximum benefit from your effort always invest your time at the most appropriate time

There are clearly times when we are much more productive, and other times when we are not nearly as productive. To maximize the impact of our time investment we should therefore work on the things of greatest long-term importance to us when we know we are going to be at our most productive.

Four things affect our productivity and effectiveness at any given time:

- our energy level

Use time or it will use you

- our state of mind, and motivation for working on this task at this time
- current level of interruption and distraction
- our level of planning; how well organised we are to get the job done

By being sensitive to these factors, and by planning and taking action accordingly, we can maximize the effectiveness of our time investments.

There is also a second interpretation of this law. It relates to the longer term and to choosing appropriate long-term goals. In some cases, the value of a g al depends very much on when it is achieved. Some people try to achieve goals either ahead of their time or when it is too late. There is the famous case of the nineteenth century mathematician and inventor Charles Babbage who tried to build a mechanical device that resembled modem day computers. Unfortunately we had to wait another century before a more appropriate technology (electronics) was available to allow viable computers to be constructed. In a similar way, being first with something can sometimes lead to success whereas a later version is not nearly so successful. Movies are a classic case where this happens.

Law 14: Invest the right amount of time

As a general rule, when working on a long-term goal, if we invest too little time in a given uninterrupted session, or we work at a goal for too long in a given session, the return on our investment will be less than directly proportional to the time invested. Put simply, from the point of view of effectiveness, we can spend too little or too much time working on a particular goal. This law is a manifestation of the more general law of diminishing returns.

The rate of progress wanes when too little or too much time is invested at one time.

Frequent interruptions are the great killers of the effective use of time. Whenever we work on something, and we are interrupted, or we interrupt ourselves, it always takes a certain amount of start-up time (15 minutes or more for most situations) to get back "into it" and to begin working productively again. Quality time is, only and always, uninterrupted time spent.

While, on the surface, spending long uninterrupted sessions working on a goal seems like a good idea, it does not always work out that way. This is particularly so, if our goal involves a considerable amount of creative work. After a substantial period of time, usually about two hours (or less) at a stretch, most people start to lose their momentum and their intensity. They also start to lose their proficiency and they start to make mistakes or not do things as well as when they started. Both a physical and a mental break is needed before we can plunge back into what we are doing with enthusiasm and efficiency. The well-known English author and politician, Jeffery Archer, has an effective approach. He is quoted as saying that he uses a two-hours-on-two-hours-off strategy when he is writing. That is, he starts writing at 6am, works until 8am, then has a two-hour break before writing for another two hours. He keeps up this pattern of work until 8pm.

Law 15: Compose activities wisely

Many people waste or lose lots of precious time unnecessarily because they do not think carefully about how they compose or adjoin the different activities they undertake or participate in each day.

Time slips away from those who fail to carefully compose their activities.

Time is lost because of the significant time gaps that exist between finishing one activity and beginning to work effectively on the one that follows it.

It is perfectly reasonable for there to be gaps between the activities that we perform each day. We need to use such gaps to socialize, to discuss things with others, and to have a break. However, these requirements aside, there are often longer gaps between activities, and more gaps than we need. Our gaps end up as time wasted.

If we become conscious of this situation, we can, over the course of a week, accumulate considerable amounts of extra time that would otherwise be wasted. The key to not wasting gap time is to plan ahead and become much more conscious of what we do.

There are two kinds of situation that we must deal with. Those where we have control over when the next activity will start and those where we must depend on others. When we are not dependent on others to start an activity the best way to avoid unnecessary gaps is to have a prior written plan which defines how long each gap should be and when we intend to start the next activity. All we have to do then is follow through and implement our plan. The situation is more difficult where we depend on others to start the next activity. In such cases, if it is a situation where we are familiar with the behavior of the group/person we can avoid wasting time by adapting to their behaviour. If it is a meeting where people chat for the first ten minutes before getting down to serious business then we can turn up ten minutes late. Where we are uncertain about the situation it is always good to bring a small piece of work or something that we can read so that we don't get caught out wasting time.

There is another way in which we can avoid wasting time when composing activities. An example will illustrate the principle. Quite often when I have something substantial that I have to get written I work in the university library for several hours in the • morning if my schedule permits. What I used to do was go to my office, drop off my bag then go off straight away to the library to work. It does not take a genius to work out that it would have been far better to go directly to the library from the car park rather than via the office. IfI adopt this strategy I save fifteen minutes. If we become conscious of what we do, when we switch between activities, we will often discover ways that will save us ten minutes here, and fifteen minutes there, and so on.

Saving time between activities all comes down to planning ahead, and being more conscious of how we do things, and of how other people do things. We just need to adapt accordingly to minimize wastage of time and make best use of gaps. We need to become much more time conscious and time wise without being either neurotic or obsessive.

The economics of this sort of time saving is compelling. If you were to save, and usefully use, only roughly an extra half an hour every day then, over the course of a year this would accumulate to an extra month of working-day (8-hour) equivalents. Most people, with a little care, can find lots more than half an hour that they waste each day. The secret is saving small amounts of time over long periods which really pays off. If we become much more time-conscious this is easy to do.

Chapter 4: Managing the use of time

"Until time is managed, everything else is impossible"
Peter Drucker

Why our use of time should be managed

It is widely accepted that management of a resource is necessary to derive the most benefits from that resource. If we accept that time is a precious resource that we want to make best use of in order to continually improve the quality of our life then we should be willing to accept that it should be managed carefully, pro-actively, and strategically.

When we look at ourselves, and others around us, we see lots of examples of the fruits of not managing time effectively. The default for not paying careful attention to time is that large amounts of it ends up being wasted or expended on things that are unlikely to do much to improve the quality of our lives or to make the world a better place.

If we want to change all this for ourselves and for others then we need to set up simple, efficient, powerful and clearly defined processes and strategies. This is essential, if we are to embark on a journey of continually improving how we utilize our time to achieve strategic long-term goals.

Management, as it is used for handling time, often carries with it too much of the notion of being a responsive or even passive form of control. It assumes "these are the things that need to be done" and that we need to make the best of the situation, no matter what the circumstances. In other words, it gives us only a very weak form of control. If we view managing time in this way, we will be unlikely to achieve much of a shift in our effectiveness.

The activity of guiding our effective use of time needs to be much more pro-active and strategic. It should be about setting the pace, calling the shots and controlling the focus. If it is not, then we are likely to waste a lot of our efforts.

What managing time entails

Management efforts are often not effective because people do not have a clear idea of what management entails. The role of management is to do four specific things:

- to define and maintain the set of long-term goals that we are passionate about investing our time to achieve

- to create and maintain the time investment priorities, plans and implementation strategies to achieve our long-term goals

- to continuously measure and monitor our performance and progress towards achieving our long-term goals

- to use the measurements and other feedback from our efforts to continually improve our effectiveness in the utilization of time on a daily, weekly, monthly and yearly basis.

It is well worth re-reading and reflecting on these four crucial points. Implementing a management process built on this framework is the key to successfully using your time.

Planning and measurement of time

To manage anything effectively you must have the best possible information that is relevant to that situation. In many cases, peoples' efforts to use their time effectively come unstuck because they do not have an appropriate planning framework. The most commonly used planning device is a diary. Unfortunately, the structure of diaries is usually not well-suited for the sort of planning and measurement we need to do to achieve long-term goals. There are also a number of computer software systems for managing tasks and time. Again, in most cases, these systems are either too elaborate or impractical for really effective planning and measurement of time.

What we need to set goals, to effectively plan, to measure our use of time and to chart our progress is a system that is very, very simple and easy to use. We need to be able to quickly represent and see at a glance:

- what we need to do, and

- what we have already done on a daily and weekly basis.

The system described below is designed to fulfil these needs. It may be implemented either as a paper-based system or preferably on a computer that you have constant access to. In my own case, I keep my planning system on a laptop computer which always travels with me.

A simple set of templates are used to manage time, set goals, allocate time to tasks, and measure progress -the latter, which provides the feedback, is critical to successfully using the system. The main template consists of a two-dimensional table (*TIME-table*) like the one shown below.

Week 48 - Nov 20 to Nov 26								
GOAL	MON	TUE	WED	THU	FRI	SAT	SUN	TOT
RENG	95	815-10						
DEG								
SQP								
DOS								
PGSQ	110	15-1700						
COD								
ADSE								
ORBK		20-2130						
OTHR	65	1030-12						
TOT	270							

EFFIC RUN %%%	MON	TUE	WED	THU	FRI	SAT	SUN	TOT
	90%							

The way I use this *TIME-table* is as follows: The first column "GOAL", contains a list of abbreviations for long-term projects and activities that I am working on, or that I plan to work on, over the next couple of years. At anyone time, I am working on about three long-term projects plus the three subjects that I teach. For example, RENG is a

Use time or it will use you

research paper I am working on, PGSQ is a book and DOS is another book that I plan to do. The row RENG allocates slots for the days of the week and the last column shows the total time in minutes I have spent on that task for the week. A student would use this table differently. They would replace some of these long-term goals by the subjects they are studying. An athlete may replace goals by the different types of training or cross-training they need to do, and so on. The important message here is that this framework is adaptable to a myriad of different applications and contexts -you need to formulate the one that suits you best. This table facilitates three critical things for using time effectively: quick and easy prioritized planning, measurement and recording, and feedback.

At the end of each evening, I sit down with my **TIME-table** and plan the times I want to spend on each major goal/project the next day. In doing this, I put in the time/duration when I intend to work on each goal. For example, for Tuesday 21st I intend to work from 8.15am until 10am on the RENG paper. When Tuesday comes along, I hopefully do the work at the time allocated and replace the time-slot 8.15-10 by how many minutes I spent on the task that day. You can see above that the time slots have been replaced by actual times-spent (in bold) for the Monday column. At the bottom of the column for each day, I add up how much time was spent on goal-related work (apart from lectures, meetings, seeing students, and administration, etc which I never bother to include in this table). For me a 100% rating is achieved if I get to spend 5 hours on productive long-term goal-related work in a day -I also never include any reading (which I do quite a lot of) in this time. In my position, I find it very hard to get the 5 hours each day given all my other commitments. However it is what I am always striving for. I use the stop-watch on my watch to measure my time spent on tasks. I start it whenever I start a new task. I think I have had a good week during semester if I get much over 25 hours done, although occasionally I crack 30hrs.

That's about all there is to it. It is a very simple, easy to use system, and it works! It takes up to one month of disciplined effort to develop the habit of using this system effectively. If you do, you will be amazed how much more you can accomplish. I have found this system much better than more elaborate commercial systems. The *TIME-table* is designed to exploit the Hawthorn effect -"we change our behaviour when things are measured" and "what gets measured gets done". I have found this to be so -I learned it the hard way. My only regret is that it took me so long to learn something that is so simple and obvious, and yet so powerful and useful.

The other key part of the system consists of four components: Meeting/Deadlines, ToDo's, Week Goals and Month Goals. Again this set up is pretty well self-explanatory. I can see all this information at a glance. It is also very easy to update. This makes for a practical system.

Use time or it will use you

MEETINGS+DEADLINES		WEEK GOALS
20 Nov Mon DM's Seminar		- Quality Metrics (120)
20 Nov Mon 1.30pm Tracy's Sem		- Re-engineering (300)
21 Nov Tue 10.30 SQI Meet		- DOS (500)
22 Nov Wed Rates $368.20		- PGSQ (500)
22 Nov Wed 4.00pm GW 234 5041		
23 Nov Thu 8.30 SPICE		
23 Nov Thu 4.30pm QC - Council Rm		
24 Nov Fri 2pm Hons Brd Fac Mt Rm		
24 Nov Fri DIST Reply		
TO-DOs		**MONTH GOALS**
*	- Robert - 0418 745524	Finish PGSQ
*	- DIST re partic Euro Proj	Finish RENG
*	- Process Engineer Arrange	DOS - 20hrs Ch 1
0	- Danny - Project	Finish Qual Matters
0	- Debra D - Qual Matters	
0	- G M-PASE	
0	- Harry F 279 4886	
0	- Kim Project	
0	- Mike D - Radiator	
0	- Order Rational Rose	
0	- Reply Leon	
0	- Res Office - PASE	
0	- Write to TY	
A	- Arrange Scholarships	
Y	- Order Writ. Sol. Code-S. Maguire	

The first column of the ToDo component perhaps needs some explanation. The "*" indicates that the task is a priority one that I need to deal with first when processing my ToDo's. The "0" means I have not attended to the task yet. The "A" means it is a task that I have actioned but that I need to do a follow up to make sure it happens. The "Y" means I have done it and can forget about it. I use the SORT function on my word processor to bubble priority items (*) to the top and re-action (A) and completed items (Y) to the bottom.

When I have finished with a particular week I just append a new copy of the templates on the front of the file and copy any leftover To Do's etc. I am then set up for the new week.

The **TIME-table** and supporting table allows me to keep track of my time on a weekly basis throughout the year and to manage and keep track of all that I need to do. I also keep three other separate files. One is called "N ext Week" which contains in chronological order all my upcoming commitments, meetings and travel, etc. At the end of each week I just cut from the top of this file those meetings etc that apply to the next week. Another file contains my goals for the year and in which month I am committed to achieving each of these goals . I look at my "Year Goals" file at the end of every month and update it as necessary. The final file I use is my LTG or "Long Term Goals" file which contains details of what I want to achieve over the next three to five year period. I look at this file every three months. At the end of June and at the end of each year I thoroughly review this file and update my long-term plans.

Below is a sample week. The example is one where I was pretty productive by my standards. I have now moved away from the idea of trying to work on more than four things in a day. By the same token I hardly ever work on a single task for a whole day -I find this not very productive. I have found it best to change after about 90 -120 minutes. Also I usually try to work on goals as much as I can in the morning, preferably starting very early. After 2pm I try to schedule meetings and other busy work etc. It does not always work out this way but this is what I aim for.

Use time or it will use you

Week Feb 27 - Mar 5th - 32 Hrs								
GOAL	MON	TUE	WED	THU	FRI	SAT	SUN	TOT
IEEE	730-930							
SE-L	45	60	30	70	52	257		
SE-W	40	45	20	30		135		
PGSO	120	90	12		60	70	10	362
COD	60	110	10-11	65	120	73	185	613
BEYP		60		60	45	75		240
ORBK	50	60	45	20		15	55	245
OTHR		20	10	35			15	80
TOT	315	445	117	280	277	233	265	1932

EFFIC	MON	TUE	WED	THU	FRI	SAT	SUN	TOT
%%%	105	146	39	93	92	78	88	91%

You will note that sometimes there are times allocated (e.g 7.30-9.30 Monday) where things don't get done. I try to fight this all the time but sometimes I don't live up to my plans. My only excuse is that I do a lot of other things as well as work on my long-term goals.

I think that's about it. Give this scheme a try and see if it works for you ¬it works for me. Since I have been measuring and planning using this system I have become a lot more productive than I ever was before. I have also become a lot more relaxed and less frustrated because I can see that I am making headway with my long-term goals. I use the laws of time investment and time utilization to guide the use of this system.

The important thing in using this system is not to necessarily expect to be very productive the first day or week you try it. It can take up to a month, or even more, to hit your straps and use the system consistently and effectively. Good Luck!! I am confident the system will work for you too and that it will not saddle you with a lot of unnecessary bureaucracy.

Improving Your Utilization of Time

This book, and others on time management, usually contain lots of suggestions about how to improve your utilization of time. The problem is that it is difficult to suddenly try to apply all these suggestions at once ¬most who try come unstuck, get frustrated, and give up any serious attempt to make better use of their time.

To avoid this sort of outcome we must recognize that effective use of time is a skill, like riding a bike or swimming -we get better at it with sustained practice and by not trying to change or master too many different things at once. No one would expect to become a champion swimmer overnight, or in a short time, even if they knew all the things that they needed to do to achieve their goal. The same applies to learning how to effectively use your time.

It is important to recognize that there are three key ingredients to improving our use of time:

- we must put in place a measurement scheme that enables us to measure and track our performance and improvements over a sustained period of time
- we must find a way to break the bad time-use habits we have and, at the same time, securely establish new, good, time-use habits

- we must find a way of breaking up the problem so that we can work towards optimizing our use of time in a systematic stepwise manner.

Motivation coach Anthony Robbins gives the sound advice: repetition is the mother of skill. There is a corresponding piece of advice for improvement: feedback is the mother of improvement. In the previous section we have suggested a simple framework that we may use to measure our progress and obtain feedback on our improvements. My strong advice to you, if you are committed to making substantial improvements in your use of time, is that you will need to implement a measurement programme. Without one, it is very unlikely that you will make either substantial or sustained improvements in your use of time. To be successful your measurement programme will in turn need to be backed up by a concerted campaign that focuses on your time usage habits.

Role of habits in improving time skills

It is what we do on a regular basis which governs whether or not we use our time strategically and effectively. It is habits or behaviours, both good and bad, that we repeatedly use which largely govern whether or not we use our time effectively.

Given this situation, if we want to improve our use of time, we will need to get rid of a number of bad habits and, at the same time, establish a number of new, good habits. This is something that is very easy to say, but much harder to do.

The human race's record on breaking bad habits is not very good. We only have to look at the struggles most people have with losing weight or giving up smoking. The reality is that bad habits usually cost us very little will-power to form and, once they are formed, they take lots of will-power and effort to break or give up.

To some degree, the situation with good habits is the opposite. Good habits can take a lot of will-power to establish and they are usually relatively easy to give up or stop practising. However, there is something else about good habits that we need to understand. An example best makes the point. Lots of people these days, at some point in their life, decide they will try running to get fit. Many of them fall by the wayside after a few days or weeks. But there are others who stick at their running year after year. Why does this happen? The answer is relatively straightforward. After running for a certain amount of time, those who do it regularly, and conscientiously, start to feel the real benefits of being fit. Once this threshold is passed the habit is established and relatively secure. The runner is no longer prepared to give up the benefits he/she gets from running. A similar thing happens with forming and using of good time utilization habits. Those who are patient enough to stick with things until the benefits start to flow are rewarded.

Breaking bad habits -building good habits

Recognizing intellectually that we have a bad habit, or that we need to establish a good habit, is not enough to bring about the necessary change. If it were, then people would

Use time or it will use you

have no trouble losing weight and so on. There is however a very simple and effective device we can use to make habit-changing work. The device relies on the Hawthorn Effect which, as we learned earlier, says people change their behaviour when it is measured. What we need to do is create for ourselves a small checklist of the bad habits we want to eliminate and the good habits we want to develop. Next to these lists of habits we build a list of eight columns -one for each day of the week plus one for totalling up our score for the week.

BHABIT	MON	TUE	WED	THU	FRI	SAT	SUN	TOT
TOTAL								
GHABIT								
TOTAL								

We can put this **Habit-auditing table** to work for us in the following way. At the end of each day we do an honest evaluation of how we have performed in relation to each of the bad habits and good habits on the list. If we have not used the bad habit for the day we put a tick in the appropriate box. If we have, we leave the box empty. Similarly for the good habits we want to develop, we use a tick when we have applied the good habit on a given day. Our goal obviously, at the end of the week, is to have all sevens in our totals. The good habits that we develop translate into invaluable time utilization skills that will enable us to use our time more effectively.

Once we have dealt with one set of habits we can start working on another set. The secret in doing this is not to work with too many different habits at once. Focus is what can make this scheme work for us. It is much better to start by having a number of small victories at the outset. These small successes encourage and motivate us to progress further.

This scheme applies very simple principles of measurement and feedback. We need to keep using this table until we are satisfied with our performance. It could take several months to completely get rid of a bad habit. Once a habit is eliminated we then just need to do a reassessment every three or four months. This will ensure that none of our bad habits have re-emerged and that our good habits remain strong. The best way to do this is to keep your old weekly habit-tables and recycle them after several months.

You can use this "technology" not only for improving your time utilization but also for changing many other aspects/behaviours of your life. *Remember, it is what you focus on, that you improve.* With any undertaking, focus, regular application, and commitment, are vital to success.

Time Utilization Maturity Model

There are a number of different things we need to do to optimize our use of time. However if we try to do all the things we need to do at once we are likely to choke on the amount of change required and either abandon the effort or end up not doing things properly. It is in this sort of situation where a maturity model can help. Maturity models have been successfully used in a number of disciplines. A maturity model acts like a ladder which we can climb one step at a time. Only when we are securely functioning at one level do we take the steps necessary to reach the next level. Such a model maps out how we can go about improving our performance in a measured, manageable, systematic way. The strength of such models is that they allow us to build incrementally on small successes. The practices at the higher levels of performance require practices at lower levels to be in place before we can expect to derive the full benefits from their use.

The maturity model described below is, by no means, one that is perfect or appropriate for everyone. It is proposed as a guide that we can use to develop a personalized model that fits our individual needs and values. If we are to maximize the benefits from our efforts to improve our use of time, we need to map out a plan. We also need to identify good and bad practices and have some sort of framework against which to benchmark our performance and the progress we make.

The maturity model we will employ consists of five levels. The lowest level of maturity reflects the weakest capability, while higher levels are intended to reflect the use of progressively more effective behaviour. We will now describe the five levels of the maturity model in terms of behaviours/practices that people might employ or exhibit when operating at a given level. To be functioning at a given level a person needs to be using all the good practices and avoiding all the bad practices that should be absent at that particular level.

While no proof exists, we claim, on the basis of observation, that if tests were done using the assessment model below most people would be found to be operating either at level one or two -which is a long way from using time effectively.

Note: In describing the model a (+) is used to indicate that an activity has reached its optimum level. Any activity that reaches its optimum level automatically promotes through to all higher levels of maturity. For example, the practice: *a diary, or related tool, is consistently used to record appointments*, reaches maturity at level 2. What this means is that the practice is also consistently used at levels 3, 4 and 5. When an activity first reaches maturity it is shown in **bold italics**. There are no mature activities at level 1.

Level 1: Chaotic

- Either no conscious long-term goals exist or, if they do, they are only vaguely formulated

- Plans, if they exist, are never written down and they are not used consistently to guide the investment and utilization of time

- No recognizable processes or techniques are used to control the investment and utilization of time

- Time is either not invested on long-term goals or, if it is, it is not invested on a regular or systematic basis

- No self-imposed deadlines or milestones are associated with tasks or long-term goals
- The majority of activities undertaken are conducted on a reactive basis
- The majority of decisions about what to do next, or of what to do at a particular time, are largely determined by others or by external factors.
- There is no on-going conscious goal-setting, or review of progress, or of goals
- No diary or related tool is used to record appointments, etc.
- Some or all of the time-wasting habits and practices identified in Appendix 1 and 2 (sections 1 and 2) are exhibited
- There is no accountability for the expenditure of time

Level 2: Immature

- Daily and weekly goals might exist but they are not systematically written down, acted on, or reviewed on a regular basis.
- Long-term goals exist but are not written down
- Time investment on long-term goals is irregular and much less than 10% on average, per week

Use time or it will use you

- Deadlines or milestones are associated with tasks but not with long-term goals
- Urgent tasks and day-to-day commitments and activities take precedence over investments of time in strategic long-term goals.
- Most time is spent on things that need to be completed within less than one week.
- Some plans exist, and are written down, but they are not consistently used to prioritize and guide the investment of time.
- To-Do lists are sometimes used to record required actions
- *A diary or related tool is consistently used to record appointments, etc (+).*
- Actions are predominantly driven by others and by external deadlines
- There is no regular use of prioritization.
- There is no attempt to control interruptions
- There is no attempt to measure the use of time on long-term goals
- There is no active effort to eliminate time-wasting habits and cultivate effective time-use habits.

Level 3: Defined

- *Daily, weekly and monthly plans and goals are written down and reviewed (+).*

- *Long term goals exist and are written down (+)*

- Time investment in long-term goals is planned but not always carried out -less than 10% on average per week is invested in LTGs

- *The use of time on long-term goals is measured (+)*

- The time spent on things that need to be completed within less than one week no longer completely dominates.

- *Recorded deadlines and milestones are associated with tasks and with long-term goals (+)*

- Actions are no longer dominated by others and by external deadlines.

- There is some use of prioritization but it is not totally successful

- *To-Do lists and diaries etc, are consistently used to record required actions (+)*

- There are attempts to control interruptions, but they are neither completely effective, nor consistently used

- Time-wasting habits are identified and are being actively worked on
- New effectiveness habits are defined and being actively cultivated.

Level 4: Managed

- *Long, medium and short-term goal setting, review, and refinement is regularly practised (+)*
- *Time investment in long-term goals is planned, carried out, and measured -at least 10% of time, on average per week, is invested in LTGs (+)*
- *The time spent on things that need to be completed within less than one week is controlled (+)*
- *Interruptions are consistently and effectively controlled (+)*
- *Prioritization of long-term goals and other activities is regularly practiced (+)*
- *Task-time estimation practiced (+)*
- Eighty percent of planned tasks, etc, accomplished weekly
- Ideal day performance achieved at least 80% of the time (e.g. 4 days out of 5). The concept of Ideal Day Performance (IDP) is discussed in the next chapter.

- *Time-wasting habits are under control (+)*
- *Time-effectiveness habits actively used (+)*

Level 5: Optimizing

- *Long-term goals given highest priority and reserving their planned, invested time commitment, on a regular basis (every day) (+)*
- *Time Investment performance is running at 100% of planned for 9 out of every 10 days (+)*
- *Ideal Day accomplishments achieved every day (+)*
- *Time is invested regularly in looking for ways to improve performance and optimize processes (+)*
- *Analysis and measurement is used systematically to support optimizing activities (+)*

In describing the Time Utilization Maturity Model I have deliberately tried not to place too much detail at each level. Each of us has different requirements and therefore we need to adapt this sort of framework to our own particular circumstances. To use the framework effectively you may need to add some detail. The thing I have tried to do, by providing this framework, is to emphasize the importance of breaking up the task of substantially improving your effective use of time. This way, there is a much greater chance of success. Using this framework conscientiously, it will take at least one month to move from one level to the next. If you try to move too quickly between levels their is a risk you will not have established a strong enough foundation to support the next higher level effectively. People operating at levels one and two should first make a concerted effort to work towards establishing the skills and behaviours that will take them to level three. The TIME-table and the Habit Auditing tables described in this chapter can help you do this. In chapter 7, a plan-of-action is given for improving your time-skills. Getting to, and being secure at a level of living that corresponds to level 5 according to the Maturity Model will, for most people, take consistent and dedicated effort over a six to twelve month period. A practical way to use this model is to set a target of two months to transition from one level to the next. Of course, the first two months should be aimed at getting to, and securely performing at level 3.

Chapter 5: Optimizing the use of time

Style is the last acquirement of the educated mind and the most useful -- A. N. Whitehead

Even when we have progressed to the stage where we are operating securely at level four or five of the Maturity Model described in the previous chapter, the job of using our time effectively is by no means finished. All we have done is created the abundance of time we need to invest to accomplish our long-term goals. Our focus should then be upon optimizing the way we do things so that we can enjoy the fruits of the effort we have invested to get to these levels. To do this we need to use a number of higher-level strategies that will help us make better choices about what we do, and about how we do these things. The two-fold aim of these strategies is to ensure we achieve our long-term goals in the most effective way and that, along the way, the quality of life we experience and generate around us, is satisfying and rewarding to ourselves and those we live, work, share and interact with.

Kipling's Profound Advice

Rudyard Kipling, famous nineteenth century novelist made the observation:

"I have six honest serving men, They taught me all I know, There names are, What and Why, And When and How, And Where and Who".

We should never underestimate the power of this question framework as a basis for planning, strategy and action, no matter what the circumstances. Asking all, or a subset of these questions: "why do xxx?, what xxx should we do?, how should we do xxx?", etc helps us to focus on the key things in any situation, whether it be sorting out our long-term goals, planning a trip or writing an essay. These questions allow us to effectively analyze and understand a situation and to structure how we will respond.

Assessing The Worthiness Of Goals

Before ever investing a lot of time in any long-term goal we need to make a thorough assessment of its worthiness. Some of the questions we should ask ourselves before committing to achieving the goal are:

Motivation

- Is the goal congruent with our value system and our more extensive set of beliefs?
- Are we motivated and excited about achieving the goal?

Significance of goal

- With this goal are we either setting our sights too high or too low? Is there a better, related goal?

- Will achieving the goal involve a substantial time investment over a long time? Unless the goal involves a lengthy investment of time it is unlikely that it will make a long-term impact on the quality of our life and those around us. In such a case we should seriously question whether it is worth doing.

- Will the process of achieving the goal and the outcome give us substantial pleasure and satisfaction?

- Is the goal something that other people feel is important or from which others will benefit?

- Is this goal the most strategic one we can choose to pursue at this time? Timing is often vital for a goal.

Cost and benefits

- What will be the cost to us of accomplishing the goal? Are we willing to pay this price and to invest the time needed to achieve the goal?

- What are the likely benefits of achieving the goal? Are these benefits we must have?

- What will be the cost of not achieving this goal? Are we willing to pay the price of non-achievement?

Long-lasting value

- If we look back on the goal, long after it has been achieved, do we expect that we will still feel that it was worthwhile.

Having made this assessment of the goal, if we are still absolutely committed to achieving it, we should start investing time in it immediately. For, as Goethe said: Whatever you can do, or dream you can do, begin it. Boldness has genius, power, and magic in it -begin it now!

We should also make sure we keep a record of this analysis which we can use from time to time when the going gets tough, when we are having doubts, or progress is slow, or we are stuck. This analysis will help to motivate us and pull us through the rough patches. And remember, every long-term project can have its low points where we doubt its worth and consider giving up on it.

On being *involved* in what we are doing

Those who race lightweight yachts seek to get their boats to a point where they are "planning". When a boat reaches this condition it literally rides on top of its own bow wave. In this state its hull displaces only a fraction of the water it does normally, so the drag generated is drastically reduced which allows the boat to increase its speed by as much as 50 percent.

What relevance has this too us? People, when they are deeply concentrating on some activity, sometimes experience a state somewhat like planning called "flow". Flow has been described as "a condition of deep, nearly meditative involvement" which can induce a sense of euphoria and at the same time result in a loss of awareness of the passage of time. People working in a state-of-flow are usually highly productive and creative.

Most of us have had the experience where we were doing something that was long and involved, but instead of struggling and wrestling with getting the job done, things just seem to flow. We have a feeling of tremendous power and we just breeze through what we would normally have anticipated would take us ages. Artists, writers and designers often claim to work in this state. My only comment is that it is well worth trying to cultivate this way of working. If we can achieve it, we will be astounded by the jump in our productivity. Unfortunately, for most of us, this state is not something we can summon at will. Our best chance for achieving it is to get really involved and focussed whenever we commit to doing anything. As one of the old Zen masters advised: when you are sitting, just sit!

A state-of-flow is the ideal state to be in when we are investing time to achieve long-term goals. To reach this level of involvement involves a transition phase. It often takes 15 minutes or more of concentrated work to enter even a mild flow state. Not everyone finds it easy to attain this state.

However with practice most of us can learn how to do it with a fair degree of repeatability.

If we are interrupted by some external event, like answering the phone, while we are in a state-of flow, it can take 15 minutes or more to get back into a flow state. For those whose work involves some sort of writing, you can easily tell when you are in a state-of-flow -the words just keep coming. You have lots more that you want to say than you are able to get written down or typed. Your brain is working in a much higher gear than your hands are able to cope with. Contrast this, to the situation where you are struggling to think what to write next -there is absolutely no flow, each word must be squeezed out and then probably it will end up being erased because you are not satisfied.

There is another aspect to "being involved" in what we are doing. It is all very well to utilize our time effectively but if the quality of the work or the outcomes we produce are not good then really our utilization of time has not been effective. For example, if we have done something only to find that we must subsequently go back and redo or fix parts of it then we are wasting precious time. Robert Pirsig, in Zen and the Art of Motorcycle Maintenance had something perceptive to say about this when describing the frustrations associated with taking a motorcycle to a bikeshop for repairs: "These were the technologists themselves. They sat down to do a job and they performed it like chimpanzees. Nothing personal in it." In his observations on the quality of work, Pirsig goes on to quote from a set of instructions for assembling a Japanese bicycle:

"Assembly of Japanese bicycle require great peace of mind". If you don't have serenity when you start, and maintain it while you are working, you are likely to build your personal problems right into the machine itself. This is why there can be problems with people's work. Their work is a reflection of their state of mind.

Doing things we don't feel like doing

There are some things that each and every one of us has to do in our job, in our domestic situation, or elsewhere, from which we derive little pleasure. This is not quite the same as being bored but it shares some of the same issues. Given that these are things that have to be done we need to ensure we use our time effectively when doing these things.

An easy job is made difficult when it is done reluctantly -- Roman Proverb

As the proverb suggests, things not done in the right spirit can be painful to do. Not only are they painful, but, more often than not, we either do them poorly and then have to do extra work to fix things up or, because of our lack of involvement, they take longer to complete than they should. Our objective in doing such things should be to find ways to make them as efficient as possible. More often than not, because these things are necessities in our work situation or elsewhere, other people will benefit or get pleasure from us doing them. For example, around our house, it is my job to do the vacuum cleaning. Even though I don't particularly like doing this domestic chore my wife is always happy when it is done. It makes the house look better, which pleases her. To make the task of vacuum cleaning more efficient I have found one strategy that cuts down the time. I always used to perform this task by taking the vacuum cleaner into each room; I would plug it in, and then clean the room. This process was repeated in each room. Stopping and starting, and plugging the cleaner in as I moved from room to room slowed the whole process down considerably. I have overcome this problem by getting a long extension cord which I plug in only once, in a central area, before I start vacuum cleaning. This cord is long enough to allow me to move from room to room without stopping -hence I have significantly cut down the time it takes me to do a task I don't particularly like.

There are two other strategies that are useful to apply when dealing with tasks that you do not particularly enjoy. The first is to always try to schedule such activities after having spent a solid amount of time working on a long-term goal that is important to you. Having accomplished something important to us, we are usually more generous with our time and able to perform, in good spirits, tasks we don't particularly like.

A strategy that many people apply with tasks that they have to do, but which they don't particularly like, is to keep putting the task off until it builds up to a situation where they have to invest a substantial amount of time to deal with it. When this happens, they resent having to spend a large amount of quality time on the task -hence the task ends up not being done in good spirits. This means the task is either not done well, or it takes longer than it should, and they end up frustrated, into the bargain. We can often overcome this sort of problem by breaking a task up into small self-contained chunks that say take no more than 10-20 minutes to do. The trick then is to regularly arrange to do one of these small activities after having invested a substantial amount of time working on a long-term goal. Obviously it would not make much sense to do the vacuum cleaning this way, but there are plenty of situations where it works very well. An example where it works very well for me is in editing a journal. I get a number of submissions coming in, or which need to be attended to, on a fairly regular basis. Each of these tasks is self-contained. What I do is take one of these tasks off to the library with me whenever I go there to spend some uninterrupted time working on a long-term goal. After I have invested my time in the long-term goal, I switch for fifteen minutes or so to attend to the editing chore. Since I have adopted this strategy I have been keeping up to date with the minimum amount of hassle. In the past, I used to let the job build up and then when it got really bad I would end up spending half a day on my editing responsibilities. I also used to begrudge this time, whereas now the job gets done almost transparently.

Maintaining momentum on long projects

It seems to be a fact of life that projects that require a large investment of time, over a long period, are always vulnerable to being abandoned. For example, many more people tell me that they are going to write a book, or that they are already writing a book than ever complete the task and get the book published. By my rough estimates at best only about one in five people complete large self-imposed tasks which they are not compelled to complete. Why projects falter is because our circumstances, our priorities and the context in which we are operating changes over any extended time period. Any, or all such changes, can put a project under threat. To make things even tougher, only some of these changes are likely to be under our controL We must therefore be well armed if we are to resist the temptation to abandon large worthwhile projects.

An important first step to protecting our large projects is having a good understanding of some of the common things that can threaten them. If we know the sort of problems that can crop up, we have a better chance of anticipating them, and equipping ourselves to deal with them, in an effective way.

Threats to projects

The threats to large projects seem to come from five main quarters:

- a change in our own or external circumstances can mean that the goal is no longer relevant or that it is no longer a priority
- other priorities, activities, or pressures arise, which compete for the time we are currently investing on working towards achieving the goal.
- we lose interest in achieving the goal

- we fail to make progress towards achieving the goal at a rate that will allow it to be achieved in a time that is relevant
- we run into technical or other difficulties associated with achieving the which or retard our

In any given situation one, or a combination of these factors, can come into play to sabotage our long-term projects.

So how do we make our projects much more resistant to such threats? There are no foolproof methods but there are number of practical things we can do.

One of the very best strategies for dealing with problems is to anticipate them in advance. At the start of a project, when we have analysed it in detail, we should try to make some sort of assessment as to what are likely to be the most significant risks to completing the project. Having done a risk analysis, we can follow it up with strategies that will help us deal with the threats, if any of them ever arise. This sort of preparation allows us to keep things in perspective and at least to have some degree of control. Threats that are anticipated usually do not sink projects. It is threats that we have not anticipated that either surprise us, or creep up on us without our knowing, which pose far greater problems.

If we do properly the sort of risk analysis suggested, it will do a lot to make our projects much less vulnerable to the five threats we have identified. On large and long projects it is a good idea to reassess our risks every three months. When this sort of risk analysis is coupled with a thorough initial project analysis we will have built a strong defence against failing to successfully complete a project.

There are also a number of other constructive strategies we can use to help keep our projects on track. These include those shown below:

Keeping projects on track

- using the guiding principles for time investment and time utilization
- making sure our goals are compelling, and clearly defined
- keeping in mind the goal and the benefits that will flow from achieving it
- developing constructive habits in relation to each goal. This includes setting regular times when we work on a project
- setting milestones and committing to achieving them
- sticking to priorities, regularly reviewing plans, and conscientiously monitoring and measuring progress never losing momentum on a project.

A common scenario with long projects is as follows. Our initial enthusiasm will usually give us the momentum that will carry us through the first ten to thirty percent of the project. It is in the 30-60% progress range with a project, that we become most vulnerable. We have made progress but our situation has possibly changed and our initial enthusiasm has been spent. Psychologically, what often happens, is that we see that there is still a long way to go and a lot more time that needs to be invested. We now know the reality of what the project is going to cost us.

It is at this time, where we must rekindle our enthusiasm and commitment to the project. If we have done our initial analysis well, this should not be too difficult. What is important to recognize is that virtually no large project goes completely smoothly, no matter how well organized, and how firmly committed we are to it. We must always be prepared to ride the bumps and to pull through the low points.

Marathon running has an important lesson for those who wish to work on long projects. Most of us have seen groups of marathon runners running along in a pack. While they stick with the pack, its group momentum tends to pull them along and make the going easier. However, if a runner drops off the end of the pack, he/she usually quickly drops a long way behind. The task of getting back onto the pack then becomes doubly difficult. A somewhat similar phenomenon seems to happen with projects. As long as we are making regular daily progress the momentum seems to feed on itself and keep us going. However, once we stop, it is like falling off the back of a pack -it can be extremely difficult to regain the momentum. I can't stress just how important this is with any large project. If there was a secret to realizing our goals it is this. Momentum is what carries us through. Lose it, and we put the project in jeopardy. And, even if the project is not lost we end up having to pay a heavy price in time, getting a stalled project back on the rails. This situation also has parallels to what happens with trains. It takes a tremendous amount of energy to get a stationary train going, relative to the amount of energy that must be expended to keep it going, once it has momentum. Remember this and make sure that you don't lose momentum on any of your large personal projects. The following diagram shows the relations between effort and progress as a function of time from the start up.

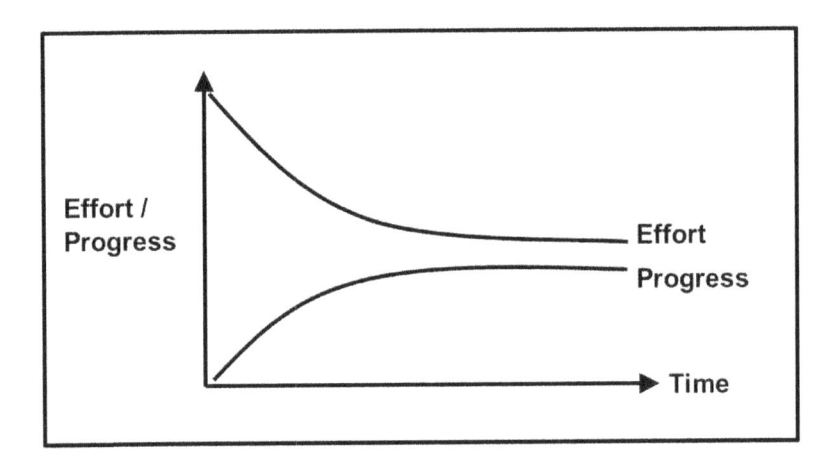

Improving the way we do things

Clearly there is more than one way to do almost any particular task we care to consider. What is more, these different ways of doing tasks, often have quite different efficiencies. Recognizing that this situation prevails is important. If we are interested in having more time to invest in long-term goals, we need to become efficiency conscious (but not neurotic or obsessive) about all the things that we do. Over a day, a month, a year or a lifetime the five minutes saved here, and the ten minutes there, adds up to a lot of time that can be put to better use.

Improvement framework

There are basically four ways we can improve any particular process:

- by using essentially the same underlying strategy but refining it by
    - deleting
    - unnecessary steps,
    - adding new steps,
    - modifying existing steps,
    - changing the order of steps, -a combination of the above
- by using the same underlying strategy but adding extra resources or a different mix/balance of resources to achieve a gain in efficiency
- by using a completely different strategy
- by deciding that it would be better to solve a different, but related, problem.

This improvement framework may be used in a completely general way. However, it is usually better to do some preliminary analysis of the situation. The first and most vital question to ask is: why do we want to improve this process, what are our overall goals and needs in this context. Also, what benefits are we seeking from the change. This additional information is often vital in guiding us on how to tackle an improvement problem. Putting a strong focus on the goal is usually the best way to improve any process.

As part of this preliminary analysis, we should also ask who, or what will benefit from the change and, who, or what, will be disadvantaged or negatively affected by the change? Almost without exception, changes have negative, as well as positive, consequences.

Rather than go into a lot of detail about how to do things more efficiently, we will use several principles and very simple examples. These are examples that probably would not occur to most people. They do, however, illustrate the spirit and intent of what might be possible in terms of time-saving.

Principle: *Always make best use of all your available resources (or use more resources to accomplish a task of fixed size in less time).*

Example (1): Both my wife and I don't care much for shopping in the supermarket but it is a job we have to do on a regular basis. What we do is always use two shopping trolleys. By deploying all our available resources intelligently, the job gets done in half the time. As a final twist, in case I finish first, I always bring a book or journal or something else to read. I used to get frustrated waiting for her to finish. Now I avoid this problem and get something useful done in the process.

This example deserves one more comment. One often sees couples pushing a trolley around the supermarket in a relaxed manner, chatting to one another, and obviously quite enjoying and sharing what they are doing. I would never advocate that people who choose to use the weekly shopping activity for relaxation adopt the alternative shopping strategy suggested above. It clearly depends on what your needs and priorities are in each particular situation.

Example (2): There are many instances where using two hands makes a difference. For example, when I put food or dishes away in the cupboard I always use two hands. This gets the job done faster.

Principle: *Always try to use (the maximum) or all the critical information when solving a problem in order to minimize effort and time.*

Example: Recently I had to replace the fluorescent light holder which had become detached from the ceiling. It had come unfastened. I tried to do the job standing on a chair. I tried for about ten minutes to slide the holder into the slots I could not see but I made no progress. The problem was that I was not high enough. This meant I was unable to see the slot that the holder fitting needed to slip into. Finally, I then went outside and got the ladder and climbed the extra foot higher. This allowed me to see the slot. I then got the job done in less than 30 seconds.

Principle: *Only perform steps that are absolutely necessary.*

Example: When I last visited my National Health Fund to make a claim, I discovered that, after more than ten years with the existing system, I no longer needed to spend five minutes filling out a form with my name and address and the doctor, etc on it. Instead I simply presented my doctor's receipt and my plastic medical card. Someone somewhere, responsible for this system, had finally decided that they already had all the information they needed on my medical card, and on the doctor's receipt, without having to generate an extra piece of paper each time I made a claim. In other words, a major step had been removed from the process, speeding it up for all concerned.

Principle: *Only change/use the number of variables that are necessary*

A powerful strategy for improving any process or task is to identify the key variables used in the process. We can then explore issues like: is it possible to establish the goal by changing less variables throughout, or by changing less variables, in a particular phase of the process? When less variables are changed, a process is simplified and, when a process is simplified, it is often more efficient.

Example The planning-writing-editing-proofing example mentioned in chapter 3 illustrates an application of this principle.

Principle: *Separate your concerns when activities are disjoint*

There are numerous instances where, given two things to do, it is more efficient to complete the first and only then attend to the second. In trying to do both at the same time we can end up frequently switching from one task to another. The switching ends up slowing down both of the tasks with the nett effect of producing a less efficient outcome.

Example: Again the example cited in chapter 3 on how to write more efficiently employs this principle. When writing, no attempt should be made to make corrections or alter the structure of the text. These tasks involve quite disjoint cognitive activities. If we keep switching between these activities, while we are trying to write, we will degrade our efficiency substantially.

Principle: Overlap tasks when they have common elements

This principle is the exact opposite of the preceding principle. Just as there are plenty of processes made up of disjoint components so too are there plenty of processes made up of overlapping steps.

Example: Suppose I need to get the paper and the milk from the corner store. It would not occur to me to go to the store, get the newspaper, come home, and then go to the store again to get the milk. Both tasks involve a common step -go to the store. While this example is very obvious there are other instances, where the overlap is not nearly as obvious. Sometimes people miss seeing common steps and end up doing things inefficiently.

Accomplishing a lot in a short time

Most of us have had occasions where a very large task just had to get done in a very short time (this discussion is for individuals working alone on something but the principles are largely the same for teams). As a general rule, we should never let ourselves get into this sort of situation. However, there are sometimes things totally beyond our control which create this situation. Therefore, when it happens, we need to be able to respond. What follows here are a set of suggestions that may be used to get a task done that involves the application of considerable mental effort over a short time. For tasks of a physical nature things are somewhat different although a number of the underlying principles are the same.

Planning

- have a clear idea about what must be done - plan, plan. Put a major effort into planning and writing down your plans and the milestones to be accomplished along the way. This will keep you focussed, and minimize time-wastage later.

- as part of your plan, make an assessment of what factors could threaten your effective use of time -then put in place what is necessary to eliminate ,or at the very least, minimize them.

- have a clear plan of what you are going to accomplish in each two hour session. Firm up your plan for what is to be accomplished in the next session during your break time. Assess your progress, and reVIse your plan and your milestones, in each break.

Doing

- throughout each two hour session remain focussed on the primary task -do not interrupt yourself. If you have distracting thoughts keep

Use time or it will use you

a note-pad nearby so that they can be jotted down and attended to later.

Having the energy to get the job done

- make sure you are not tired to start with
- eat only fruits with high water content. Eat every two hours to keep up your energy -don't eat anything heavy like meat, etc as it uses up a lot of energy for digestion and makes you sleepy.
- during your break time, do the following breathing exercise: breath in deeply through your nose for five seconds, hold your breath for twenty seconds and breath out for ten seconds. Repeat this process ten times. It oxygenates your blood and at the same time helps to more effectively remove waste products from your blood stream. As a consequence you should have more energy.
- drink plenty of water so that you don't become dehydrated during a session. If you become dehydrated, you can end up with a headache which will stop you from working effectively.
- alternate with half hour and one hour breaks every two hours (sometimes it can make sense even to have a two-hour break between sessions) . Do not try to work intensively for more than two hours at a stretch, if you want to

remain effective, and avoid feeling stale or restless.

- go for a walk and do some exercise in your break time and perhaps have a shower to relax you and freshen you up.

Creating the right working environment

- create an environment or situation where there will be n 0 interruptions, no telephones, etc
- try to have good natural light and fresh air
- make sure your working environment is slightly on the cool side, but not uncomfortably cold, because the cold can distract you
- put some peppermint oil or other air refreshing substance in the room
- make sure you have plenty of space, and a chair that gives good back support
- before starting each two hour session, make sure you have all the facilities you will need. This ensures you do not have to move in that time

If you follow this set of guidelines you will be amazed at what you can accomplish in four or five sessions in a single day.

For a team working on a large project, that must be done in a short time, most of the same guidelines apply. However, much more effort must go into planning and communicating in break times.

Before finishing off this section it is worthwhile noting the working pattern that best-selling author, Jeffery Archer, uses:

Start work at 6am and work until 8am, Have a two hour break, Start work at 10 am and work until 12noon Have a two hour break, Start work at 2pm and work until 4pm Have a two hour break, Start work at 6pm and work until 8pm

Smelling the roses along the way

Each human being is a lot like a garden. When we are young we have a sense of adventure, and a great diversity of interesting things, within us. However, if our metaphorical garden is to flourish, in our lifetime, it must be frequently nurtured, nourished and cultivated. Without plenty of care many of the things that we treasured when we were young whither up and die.

Looking back on his life, and on his achievements, Charles Darwin, proposer of the theory of evolution, was prompted to make the remark:

"If I had my life to live again, I would make it a rule to read some poetry and to listen to some music at least once every week. The loss of these tastes is a loss of happiness."

Darwin's message is clear. If we are to live a life that will give us long-lasting pleasure and satisfaction, then we should see to it that our life has balance. There are extremes ranging metaphorically from "all work and no play" through to "all play and no work". Neither of these alternatives is very attractive for the quality of life that they give us, both in the short-term, and in the longer-term. If we become obsessive about achieving a long-term goal at the expense of the quality of the life that we must live until the goal is accomplished then, by the time the goal is accomplished, other things in our life, that give it quality, may have been lost or destroyed along the way. And, as a consequence, we may have lost what it takes to enjoy life.

What is worth striving for in living is not to end up in a situation where, later in our life, we regret not having done a lot of things along the way that were within our reach and which would have made a difference to the quality of our life both in the shorter term, and in the longer term. It is what we do, on a day-to-day basis, that gives meaning and quality to our lives. We cannot expect to neglect things for long periods and then rekindle them with the same vitality. In other words, the journey should be as good as arriving.

A lot of what it takes to live a happy and fulfilling life comes down to continually striving to know more about ourselves, what we like, what makes us happy, and what we want to achieve in the longer term. We can only discover these things if we are continually learning about ourselves and growing. We must see beyond being totally absorbed in day-to-day affairs, but at the same time, we must not neglect the quality associated with the way we live each day.

Living an ideal day every day

Imagine we could live a day as though all that we wanted to do and experience happened in that day. What are all the things that would be on our list? It is very illuminating to construct such a list. People rarely contemplate such things because they seem impossible. By doing such an exercise, we learn a lot more about ourselves. It is also useful to ask this question about a longer time period, a month or a year. We should do this periodically.

The ideal day, month and year exercises are very useful as inputs to our goal-setting and our short and long-term planning processes. They can be used for assessing our performance, and for choosing what to do that will give us long-lasting pleasure and satisfaction. The structure and activities that we come up with should be derived from and/or compatible with our core values and beliefs.

Sometimes the thing that really makes a day involves doing some little thing for someone we have never even met before. Some time ago, I was travelling on a crowded train to Heathrow Airport in London. At one of the stations along the way, an old lady struggled onto the train with a heavy bag. She moved to a position where she could hold onto an upright near the door and caught her breath. As she did, a young black man quickly got to his feet and offered her his seat. I am sure the old lady, who was white, was surprised, as were the rest of the people in the crowded carriage. The old lady accepted the offer graciously, and sat down. No one said anything, they just pretended to mind their own business. However by that simple, spontaneous and generous act, that young man completely changed the atmosphere in the carriage. That incident had a lasting impact on me, and probably also on a number of others on that train. I am not sure how the young man felt about what he had done, but he was certainly playing his part to make the world better for us all. If we can all do our share of unexpected little things for other people, as part of our ideal day plan, the world can only get better. Such little ripples of care, if there are enough of them, can turn the tide of alienation, unfriendliness and loneliness, that many people experience in the hustle and bustle and chill of modern life.

If we were able to live according to our ideal day each and every day, we would be truly happy and satisfied with our lives. Of course, in many instances, it will be very difficult for us to completely realize our ideal on a daily basis, for a whole variety of reasons. What is important however, is that we have an ideal to aim for, whatever our circumstances. No matter how bad or good the circumstances, there are things we can do to make the very best of the situation. The value we should strive to live by is:

to live each and every day in the very best possible way we can.

It is so easy to fall into the habit of not living our life to the full. We hope that at some unspecified future time things will be better, and that we will be able to do all the things we wanted. Rarely do things work out this way for people.

Barbara Cartland gave some good advice on how to live each day.

There is an unlimited power in life, whether one believes it is divine or human in origin, what matters is that it is there to be used -- Barbara Cartland

A somewhat more extreme suggestion is to say we should live each day as though it were our last, or as Thoreau said:

Our life is frittered away by detail... simplify, simplify!

And to finish, Socrates profound advice: let no day pass without discussing goodness obviously needs to be part of any ideal day.

So what may we hope to achieve in an ideal day, where we use our time strategically, passionately and compassionately. The following is a list we could start with:

- Our time investment performance is running at 100% of planned
- Ideal Day accomplishments achieved
- Learning goals satisfied
- Health and fitness goals satisfied
- Family/relationship goals satisfied
- Have done at least one creative thing
- Have done at least one unexpected thing to make someone happy
- Have done at least one thing to make the world a better place

When we are making steady and regular progress on our long-term goals it usually has the effect of making us feel much more relaxed. The feeling of constantly being busy disappears and we feel much more in control of our lives and of our own destiny. This in turn leads to a sense of growing pleasure and satisfaction -this is where we want to be in terms of the way we live our lives. This is what the strategic use of time is all about. Without a goal and a commitment to live an ideal day every day how can we expect to improve the quality of our lives.

In practical terms for each and every day, given our circumstances and commitments, we should get up in the morning with the intent to live an ideal day. This requires planning and action in terms of time investment and accomplishment. It may also help to construct a generic "ideal day" for each day of the week. We can then make minor modifications for a given day to accommodate our commitments, which are particular to that day. This cuts down the amount of planning we need to do. While this may sound a lot like putting us in a very "planned" straight-jacket it is certainly not the intent. The spirit of what we are trying to convey is that each of us should strive with full-on commitment to have the best possible day we can each and every day of our lives. This won't happen if we cut comers on quality and planning or we sacrifice our commitment to balance and to helping and sharing with others. It is what we do, on a daily basis, that brings quality to the way we live. Quality is not some vague nebulous ideal we hope to achieve at some unspecified time in the future when" we vainly hope things will get better and we will be under less pressure". Our commitment to achieving quality in our lives, no matter how modest, must start now! Remember Aristotle's profound advice: we are what we repeatedly do. Every day is equally important if we are interested in improving the quality of our life.

In proposing the idea of an ideal day we are not suggesting that, even according to our own terms, we have such days very often, if at all. The whole point is to set a goal, or a standard to which we can aspire. Without having something like this to aim for it is hardly likely we will ever make much consistent progress towards improving the quality of our days and ultimately the quality of our life.

Once we have set such a benchmark for ourselves, we can develop the habit of spending a few minutes each evening reviewing what we could have done better to have given ourselves, and others, greater pleasure and satisfaction. It may help to record any actions, changes, etc, we need to make to the way we do things so that next time, when confronted with a similar situation, we will take action or respond in a way that would have made the day a better one by our new standards. Some people may also find it helpful to keep their Ideal Day Performance analyses in a diary and review them periodically, to check whether they are improving, optimizing and getting better at all that they do. Feedback guides, and drives, improvement. And, what we choose to focus on, provided we are persistent and consistent, is where we get the results and the return on our investments. This seems to be an inescapable fact of life. The decision is ours, the ball is in our court.

Chapter 6:
Time and your future

Your future depends on every day that passes -- J.D. Rockefeller

In the discussion of the strategic use of time two fundamental questions have been addressed:

1. *How can we decide on what we should use our time for if we wish to live a life that will give us long-lasting pleasure and satisfaction?*

2. *How can we create the abundance of time we need to invest to accomplish the things that will give us long-lasting pleasure and satisfaction?*

I assert that there are four things we need to use our time strategically for:

- to achieve long-term goals
- to pursue life-long learning and personal growth
- to assist others and contribute to society
- to maintain our health and fitness.

How do we know that this is the right combination for everyone? My response to this is to say that such a question is probably the wrong one to ask. There is however a prevailing view, dating right back to the Ancient Greeks which says that a balance in life is what gives it quality.

If, for instance, we choose not to use at least some of our time to achieve long-term goals then what are we sacrificing? The answer is, we will never know if we have not tried. Certainly most, if not all, those who have tried and achieved worthy long-term goals would, on balance, strongly support and advocate such a strategy. What is more, another simple test we can apply is to ask ourselves who in the world today, or in the past, we admire or wish we were like. My guess is that, more often than not, it will be people who have achieved worthy long-term goals. Failing to take up the challenge is cutting off a part of our experience that each and every human being should explore. Not everyone of us can be a Shakespeare, a Mozart, an Einstein, a Mother Teresa, a George Bums, a Steven Spielberg or a Mark Spitz. However, there are plenty of things within our reach that will give us long-lasting happiness if only we have the courage to reach out and take up the challenge. Following such a path is our best insurance for living a full life, and for not waking up one day to the realization that we have wasted so much of the potential that we had. We do not want, on reflection, to come to the conclusion that life has, for us, always been like a river, where we have sat on the bank and watched as a spectator instead of having dived in and felt its power and experienced its delights.

We can treat each of the other three strategic uses of time in exactly the same way as long-term goals. The choice of not seeking to use our time to experience and achieve them will just cut off another vital part of living life to the full. No one can compel us to do any of these things -the choice is always ours. However if our life is to have purpose and meaning then we should give serious consideration to using time to experience a balance among all these things. Remember that the greatest pleasure and satisfaction in life comes from accomplishment that contributes to the common good.

There is no question that how we spend our time affects the quality of our life NOW and in the future. While we are not advocating a preoccupation with the future or success we are suggesting that at least some of what we do now should be tied to what we want in the future. For as Paul Valery said: if you don't think about your future you won't have one.

What we have in life is a choice between optimism and action, or detachment, pessimism, inaction and passive behaviour. Without exception, all of us would prefer to live a life of better quality. However, if we choose not to try things, not to take risks, not to take up opportunities how can we expect the quality of our life or the world around us to improve? The plain reality is that it won't. Sure, some of the things we might try will not always succeed. However, the occasional failure can hardly be worse than never having tried. An attitude to life that is predominantly positive, optimistic, creative, generous, adventurous, non-egocentric and persistent in the face of failure and adversity, is superior to other alternatives. It will sometimes get us into trouble and cause us pain, but, on balance, it will lead us to a life of greater quality and happiness. If we adopt such an attitude, which is something, everyone can do, no matter what their circumstances, then we will have the commitment, the enthusiasm and the energy to use our time strategically. By doing so, we will improve the quality of our life and play our small part in making the world a better place. In this regard, the philosopher Bertrand Russell, gave good advice.

Use time or it will use you

A life focussed on creating rather than possessing has a far greater potential for happiness and fulfilment Bertrand Russell (paraphrased)

What we have provided in this book is a very simple philosophy and a set of strategies, tools and techniques, which, if used properly, can give each and everyone of us tremendous freedom, exhilaration and satisfaction. However, like all such disciplines, if this technology is abused or used only in a selfish or obsessive way it can make our life, and that of those around us, hell. It all comes down to a question of balance, commonsense application and thinking beyond base self-interest. We must understand this technology, and apply it with passion, sensitivity and care, to make our life better, others lives better and the world a better place. We should make ourselves masters of time, not just another of its slaves. If you have got this far with this book you have a choice to make -either to go on as before, or to CHANGE and make real improvements to the quality of your life and that of the lives of the people around you. The challenge and the technology, and all that they offer have been placed before you ¬the rest is up to you! Make time for the things that are important to you. Make things happen. Live, don't just exist. It is now time for action!

I went to the woods because I wished to live deliberately ... and see if I could not learn what it had to teach, and not when I came to die, discover that I had not lived. I did not wish to live what was not life, living is so dear -- H.D. Thoreau

Chapter 7:
A plan for action

A journey of a thousand miles always has a first step – Lao Tzu

Where do we start?

Having provided a set of guiding principles for the strategic use of time, all that remains is to provide advice and suggestions for a plan of action that will enable us to exploit these principles.

One way to interpret what has been provided thus far, is to see it as a discipline that we can employ to do things that will satisfy our current and future time investment and time utilization needs. Discipline however, is always a double-edged sword. On the one hand, little of significance is achieved without at least some discipline. On the other hand, when we employ discipline, there is always the danger of falling into the trap of focussing too much on conforming to the discipline as an end in itself. The important focus should be upon what we accomplish and the pleasure, satisfaction, freedom and the other benefits we and others derive from using discipline in a commonsense way. The intent has certainly not been to create a time utilization straight-jacket that will just add more pressure to people's lives. There always needs to be room for flexibility, spontaneity, imagination and creativity in what we do. A preoccupation with discipline can stifle these things and detract from our quality of life. It comes down to a question of balance and moderation. The suggestions which follow should be seen in this light.

The plan of action put forward is intended only as a loose guide. What suits or works for one individual, may not work as well for another, in their current situation. There is no suggestion that it has to be closely followed. In my own case, I certainly did not follow a plan that was anywhere near as prescriptive. I arrived at my current level of time utilization maturity by a longer and more painful route. The practices that I have adopted, and continue to evolve, came into place in a much less structured way.

At all times, in our planning, we should not lose sight of what we are trying to do. Our major focus needs to be on these three fundamental focus questions:

- how to utilize time to achieve our long-term goals,
- how to optimize our utilization of time, and
- how to utilize time to . of life.

Action plan

To make progress we need to formulate and implement an action-plan that involves commencing activities on two fronts:

Fundamental action strategies:

- we need to get started in broadest terms, on accomplishing the key things that will improve our quality of life, and, at the same time,

- we need to start actively improving our time-skills. These two activities are

The way you approach setting up a personal action plan will depend to some degree on your circumstances; whether it is something that you will need to implement outside your work or your family commitments; whether it can be integrated with your work or your studies or school programme; or whether some other situation applies. In the end, you will be the best judge of how a time utilization programme can fit with your situation. You may, of course, use these ideas to improve the quality of all that you do. Suggested planning for the two different types of activity will now be outlined. This will be followed by a stepwise implementation of the plan that is supported by a number of self-assessment, planning and measurement templates.

Quality of life planning

Step 1

A useful place to start would be to re-read the book now that you have a perspective on what it is trying to do. You always pick up a lot more from a second reading of any book. (If you are too "busy" to do a complete re-read then at least review chapters 2 -5. And, if you are so desperate that this is too much of a commitment, then at least review the laws summarized in STEP 1 of the Plan-For Action at the end of this chapter -after section 6).

Step 2

Once you have reviewed the book and the laws you need to do some hard thinking or personal brain-storming to identify and evaluate a set of long-term goals and quality-of-life improvements that you want to make. This is something you might need to reflect upon and refine for days, or even weeks. When you are satisfied with what you have come up with you could enter the results in the templates provided in STEP 2.

Coming to these decisions is not something you can just make happen. It can be slow and painful, particularly if you have not been used to doing a lot of strategic thinking. One way to tackle this exercise is to get a note pad or a computer file and sit down with it on a daily basis and:

- write down in point form your ideas about your future,
- about what is really important to you, and
- about what you really want to accomplish and contribute.

Trying to write things down will stimulate your thinking. You need to stick at this daily routine until you are happy with what you have created. It may help to imagine that this is a report or assignment that you need to do for your boss or your teacher, or your professor. Stick with this planning exercise until you have formulated a set of goals and changes that you are passionate about achieving. These should be things which you know will make a difference to the quality of your life. Use the guidelines in chapter 5 to assess the goals you come up with. This is all about creating a compelling future for yourself. As part of your brainstorming, some of the questions that you might address may include the following:

Strategic questions

- what do you want to accomplish and create (your goals and contributions to your family and friends and society)
- in order of importance, what set of long-term goals do you want to achieve.
- who do you want to be (what labels or roles do you want to have in life, e.g., father, lawyer, good golfer, etc)
- what do you need to do to improve the depth and quality of the relationships you have
- what values do you want to live by, in the way you behave and in the way you treat others
- what is your self-worth and what sphere of influence do you want (the broader this is, usually the more satisfaction it gives

From this long-term planning you need to work out a set of targets and milestones to be achieved within say 2-5 years and another set to be achieved within 5-10 years. This all needs to be carefully written down in a form that clearly identifies what the target is, when you want to achieve it by, and why it is important to you, your family and friends and broader community.

Step 3

The next step is to draw up a list of what quality-of-life improvements and goals/milestones you want to achieve within one year. These tasks are critical. What you set for yourself, and what you are able accomplish within one year, will largely determine whether strategically investing your time is going to have a lasting impact on your quality-of-life. The goals you want to accomplish (or make defined and measurable progress on) within one year need to be broken down further into a set of very concrete milestones, with explicit descriptions of what is to be accomplished and when it is to be accomplished by, and how much time you are prepared to invest on a regular basis (weekly/monthly). This may include a set of monthly targets (time-spent, and exactly what is to be accomplished) to be achieved over the next twelve months. The closer the target the more detail there should be on specifically what needs to be done. This plan needs to be reviewed and revised at least monthly. In my own case, I review and update my plans at the end of each calendar month. Some sample templates are given in STEP 3. You however may wish to customize a set to better suit your own particular needs.

Time skills improvement plan

Step 4

The next thing to do is conduct a self-assessment based on the time utilization maturity model described in chapter 4.7

(a template for doing this is provided in STEP 4). Before doing this assessment it would be advisable for you to re-read chapter 4.7. This self assessment should give you a reasonably clear picture of what your current level of time utilization maturity is. It should also identify some skills and problems that you can start working on. Conscientiously using the TIME-table and the Habit-Audit table alone, can do a lot to raise your time-skills. Remember, because activities at higher maturity levels depend on other activities at lower levels being in-place, it is prudent not to skip developing capabilities at the lower levels first. In this regard, famous basketballer Michael Jordan's advice makes a lot of sense. He said: I don't care what you're doing, or what you are trying to accomplish; you can't skip the fundamentals if you want to be the best.

With regard to your improvement programme, the most important thing is to decide exactly what you are going to focus on improving over the next month. How you handle this will more than likely determine whether you change forever the way you use your time or whether you give up and end up back where you started. It is foolish to be over ambitious in this regard. Remember developing good "use-of-time" habits and skills is not something that can be turned on like a tap. These skills must be nurtured and developed step-by-step with patience and persistence. Time-skills development is not something that most of us find easy to sustain. It usually represents a big change. And, big changes don't come easy -they are usually hard won, but I can assure you, well worth the effort.

Remember it is lots of small victories on a daily basis, that will, in the end, build into an enviable capability for utilizing your use of time. Of course, there will be days and maybe even weeks when you do not live up to your expectations. However, if you keep persisting, and you keep persisting, you will eventually develop the skills and habits that will make time your ally in your quest to improve the quality of your life.

Step 5

The remaining step you need to do is to identify your time problems and time-wasting habits. Appendices I and II will help with this task. The results from these assessments, together with your time utilization maturity assessment, provide the raw materials you need to develop a time utilization improvement programme with a set of goals and improvements you intend to achieve over the next twelve months. You can either use the results as is, to guide you, or you may prefer to draw up a specific improvement plan. You should do maturity assessments at least every three to six months to monitor your improvements. Initially, it is a good idea to do a new self-assessment after three months to see what headway you have made. If you are using the TIME-table and the Habit Audit Table (or their merged form) conscientiously you should see very significant improvements within three months of starting to use the system.

Use the discussion in Appendix I and II (section 2) [and the templates in STEP 5] to identify and possibly rank, in order of seriousness, your motivation and planning problems and your time wasting habits. Pick the top two or three of these habits and insert them into the weekly Habit-Auditing table or into the Timetable used in STEP 6. When I work on my habits, I review these at the end of the day at the same time as I do my planning for the next day. To make this whole thing easier you may choose to include your habit management in your TIME-table. Remember feedback is the mother of improvement and the key to both forming and breaking habits. When you have not succumbed to a particular bad habit for a period of a month, it is usually safe to stop monitoring it. It is a good idea to review the habits you need to work on at the end of each month. In forming good habits, keep in mind that repetition is the mother of skill.

Step 6

As soon as you have identified one or more long-term goals in your strategic Quality-of-Life planning you should start using the TIME-table discussed in chapter 6. Weekly templates are provided in STEP 6.

I have found it best to use this system in the following way. Each evening, last thing before I go to bed, I sit down with my computer and work out the times I plan to spend the next day working on my long-term goals. As part of this process, I also review what has been accomplished for the day and make any adjustments to my plans for the week and to my To Dos, etc. This usually takes no more than ten minutes. I have found that it is very important to plan the night before rather than in the morning. If you fail to plan for the next day in the evening there is a risk that you will get distracted in the morning, and before you know it, the day has evaporated and nothing on your long-term goals has been accomplished. Having a plan for the next day allows you to get focussed right from the outset. If you get a good start, and get quality work done on your long-term goals early, then there is a high probability that the rest of the day will go well. This process works very well for me; there is a good chance it will also work well for you. The critical thing is to make a firm commitment about when you intend to do things, particularly the work on your long-term goals. They should pretty well always have the highest priority and hence the first call on your time each day. Once they have been attended to there can be time for other things. Al ways remember just how important your long-term goals are to you.

Daily planning process

The daily process we need to employ to plan, manage and measure our time should be very simple. How we plan and prioritize our use of time should, at all times, be guided by what long-term goals we are currently working towards achieving. Our objective, in our daily planning, is always to MAKE the time to work on our long-term goals. Remember the second law of time investment -invest 10% of your time working on your long-term goals each day.

In choosing to work on long-term goals there are two important issues to settle:

- how many long-term goals should you be working on at any one time
- How much time should you work on a given long-term project on an on-going basis

circumstances and the nature of your goals. In my own experience, I have found it best to work on between two and four major long-term goals at one time. More than this, in my own case, and I find my effort gets too diluted and I start to lose efficiency. By the same measure, working on just a single goal can get boring and tiring unless it can be broken up into quite distinct parts. Probably the optimum way for me to work is to focus on only two major long-term goals at anyone time.

Just how long to spend working on each long-term goal in a day and in a week is again a very personal thing. The sort of long-term goals I work on usually involve intellectual work, like writing. For this sort of task, I find it best to work for no more than 90-120 minutes at a stretch.

Some books on time management suggest that people measure and account for all their activities and all the time they spend. This becomes tedious and a waste of time. A better strategy is to apply the Pareto Principle and only worry about planning, managing and measuring time associated with your important long-term goals. Remember it is where you focus that you get results.

Don't make the mistake of planning the whole day, each day. Leave some room for flexibility. The secret to effectively using your time on a daily basis is striking a balance between being very disciplined about the time spent working on long-term goals and being relaxed about the time spent on other things. In my own case I could, if I chose, be much more disciplined about how I spend considerably more of my time. However what suits me best, on a daily basis, is to be very disciplined about getting the quota of work on my long-term goals done first. I am then free to deal with my other responsibilities and to interact with other people. On occasions there are times when I need to be disciplined for a day or a week at a time. I adjust accordingly. However, operating in this way, enables me to feel relaxed, not under pressure, and in control of my life without being enslaved by the time utilization system I have created. The system works for me and facilitates what I do -it is neither a burden, nor a straight-jacket. As long as things are progressing well on my long-term goals the other things I do tend to fit into place and not get out of hand. I cannot do everything I would like to do but the most important things get done on a regular basis. The following set of steps may help with your daily planning.

Steps:

1. First thing in morning review the day-plan you have created the previous evening and set about working to your plan for the day. Make sure you have a firm commitment to stick to your plan, particularly your long-term goal commitments.

2. Time, and record the time spent on each long-term goal during the day (do this accurately and conscientiously as you finish working on each goal, otherwise your time measurement becomes a fiction that is of little real help). I use the stop-watch on my watch for this purpose.

3. Use your TIME-table as needed, throughout the day or evening. to record and cross off To Dos, meetings, appointments, etc.

4. Last thing in the evening, review what you have accomplished for the day on your long-term goals and other commitments and plan your next day accordingly. Also review the good/bad habits you are working on and record your progress.

Things to keep in mind each day

It is not all that hard to draw up a plan for what you intend to do on a given day. It is much, much harder to execute that plan. For most of us, there are always many things and many people to distract, hinder, disrupt and tempt us away from following through on what we have planned to do. The following are a few reminders that can help ward off these things that sabotage the best of intentions. I keep a list of these on my computer. I look at them every time I open my planning file. This helps to bring me back on track.

- value your time each and every day
- make time for the things that are important to you.
- don't put off doing things that are important to you no matter what the circumstances
- plan and prioritize how you will use your time each day
- plan the night before so that you can get stuck into things first up
- try to get work done on long-term goals early in the day when you are fresh. After a hard day it can be

hard to be effective and there is often a much greater temptation to give up before you have done the allotted amount of time..'
- always keep a focus on investing time in what is important in the long-term (apply the 10% rule, that is, invest 10% of your time each and every day in your future)
- guard your time and stick to your plan
- strive to have an ideal

Weekly planning process

At the end of each week there are two things we need to do. First review and assess what we have achieved for the week. This information can then be used to plan what we want to achieve in the next week. This all sounds very simple, and it is.

The review step is important because it allows us to gauge how effectively we are using our time. This feedback alerts us to problems. If we note carefully what this information tells us, we should be able to use it to improve our time-skills, our performance and the rate at which we accomplish long-term goals.

The planning for the next week is equally important. Two factors influence what goals we set for the next week: the progress we have made with our long-term goals over the previous week and the goals we have set for the current month. From this information we should have enough details to plan precisely what needs to be accomplished in the coming week. As part of this process we should estimate/plan how much time is to be spent on each long-term goal during the week. This information may then be used to guide the decisions we make in our day-to-day planning over the coming week. Make sure that throughout the week you regularly remind yourself what goals you have set for yourself over the coming week.

A good time to do your weekly review and planning is last thing on a Sunday evening at the time you when you do your daily planning.

Monthly planning process

The process we need to apply at the end of each month is very similar to what we do at the end of each week. We need to review what has been achieved for the month and use this to set our goals for the next month. In setting our new month-goals it is important to check against our longer term plans and milestones so that we can make any adjustments that need to be made. The goals we set should always be realistic. Many people either set goals that are unrealistic or which, in their hearts at least, they do not expect to realise. Such self-deception is of no value. Never set a goal you do not plan to achieve in the time you have allotted.

The best time to do your monthly planning is at the end of each calendar month -this is the easiest to remember. I make it a habit of doing my monthly review on the last day of each month.

Half-yearly review and annual planning

Half-yearly and annual planning is quite a different sort of planning to that which we engage in on a daily, or weekly basis, etc. It is a much more soul-searching and strategic activity. What we need to do at these times is to stand back a little from what we are doing and re-evaluate our situation, the goals we are pursuing, our rate of progress and the direction our life is taking. It is very easy to get caught up in day-to-day affairs which can lead us in directions we no longer wish to take. Also, new opportunities can arise which may mean that we need to change our focus in the way we are investing our time. Of course, opportunities do not necessarily come at six-monthly intervals. This means that sometimes, outside our scheduled review times, we need to totally reassess our situation. This aside, a six monthly review is a very worthwhile process for us all. We need it to recharge our batteries and to make sure that our enthusiasm for achieving our long-term goals is running at the highest possible level. At this point, all our current goals and ideas should be up for grabs. They may be continued, modified or scrapped, depending on the outcome of our review.

A practical way to conduct your bi-annual review is to revisit the Quality-of-Life Planning process and the Time-Skills Improvement programme set out earlier in this chapter and the results of your self-assessment and planning as described at the end of this chapter. As part of this review you need to do two key things: evaluate your progress on our long-term goals and assess how well you have progressed with improving your time-skills. This evaluation should include a time utilization assessment. In doing this you need to assess the improvements over the last six months.

I find the best time to do this review is right at the end of my holidays after I have had a break and I feel ready to tackle new things with enthusiasm. You may sit down and try to do this over a day or a half a day. What I find is that, even if I do this, other ideas keep coming up for the next few days until I settle down into a rhythm again.

All that remains is for you to start using your own personalized version of the system that has been described. In the remainder of this chapter a set of templates is provided that you may wish to use to set about the task of accomplishing your long-term goals, improving your time-skills and most importantly improving your quality-of-life. The rest is up to you ¬commit now and take sustained action over the next year and watch what happens.

Use time or it will use you

A plan for action

1. Review laws of time investment, utilisation

Time Investment Laws Summary

Law 1: **Create and Maintain a Compelling Future**
Create a compelling vision that has tangible specifications for three things: what you want to be, what you want to accomplish and what you want to contribute.

Law 2: **Invest Time In Your Future**
Accomplishment, success and satisfaction comes to those who invest at leas 10% of every day working towards the achievement of long-term goals.

Law 3: **Invest Time In Worthy Goals**
Those who invest time in worthwhile long-term projects are rewarded.

Law 4: **Time Must Be Made For Important Things**
Time must be *made* for long-term projects that are important, no matter what your present circumstances.

Law 5: **Invest Time In Personal Growth**
A part of your time is yours to invest in your own development and growth no matter what your current circumstances are.

Law 6: **Invest Time In Other People**
The greatest gift we can give another human being is our time and our undivided attention.

Law 7: **Focus on the Vital Few (Pareto)**
Beware, 20% of the time invested can yield 80% of the returns obtained, while 80% of the time invested may yield only the remaining 20% of returns.

Law 8: **The Last 20% Makes The Difference**
Between Good and the Best is a Large Effort. Situations are numerous where a 20% effort will return you 80% of what it is possible to achieve but where you will need to invest another four times that effort to be the best or to make an outstanding achievement.

Law 9: **Worthy Results Take Time**
Time slippeth away from those who expect results from their investment too quickly.

Law 10: **Avoid Useless Activity**
Never engage in useless activity.

Law 11: **Do Not Dwell on Achievement, the Past or Failure.**
Time and opportunity slippeth away from those who dwell too much on their past, their achievements, or their failures.

Use time or it will use you

Time Utilization Laws Summary

Law 1: **Value Your Time**
Those who value their time have sown the seeds to acquire gold

Law 2: **Let the Goal be the Guide**
Begin with the end in mind, continue with the end in mind, and finish with the end in mind.

Law 3: **Prioritize Your Use of Time**
Those who value their time and prioritize its use are nurturing the plant that will yield them gold

Law 4: **Plan Your Time**
Time slippeth away from those who fail to plan how they will use it

Law 5: **Stick To Your Priorities and Plans**
Gold cometh in plenty to those who consistently value their time, consistently prioritize its use wisely, and consistently stick to their priorities

Law 6: **Guard Your Time**
Time slippeth away from those who do not guard its use

Law 7: **Measure Your Use Of Time**
Those who measure their strategic use of time, improve their effectiveness

Law 8: **Use an Effective Process**
The process determines the quality of the outcome and the time expended

Law 9: **Avoid Frequent Task-Switching**
It takes less time to do n disjoint tasks separately, one at a time, from start to end, than to switch between them

Law 10: **Don't Just Twiddle Your Thumbs at Road-Blocks**
When you see a road-block, don't just sit there, take quick and decisive action.

Law 11: **Expend the Time Required**
Time slippeth away from those who try to accomplish a goal in too short a time

Law 12: **Accomplish All You can**
Time slippeth away from the person who tries to accomplish too little in a given period of time

Law 13: **Invest At The Right Time**
To gain maximum benefit from your effort always invest your time at the most appropriate time

Law 14: **Invest the Right Amount of Time**
The rate of progress wanes when too little or too much time is invested at one time

Law 15: **Compose Activities Wisely**
Time slippeth away from those who fail to carefully compose their activities

Use time or it will use you

2. Determine your medium & long-term goals

LONG TERM GOALS (5-10 YRS)	WHY THEY ARE IMPORTANT
GOAL 1:	
Complete By:	
GOAL 2:	
Complete By:	
GOAL 3:	
Complete By:	
GOAL 4:	
Complete By:	
GOAL 5:	
Complete By:	

LONG TERM GOALS (2-5 YRS YRS)	WHY THEY ARE IMPORTANT
GOAL 1:	
Complete By:	
GOAL 2:	
Complete By:	
GOAL 3:	
Complete By:	
GOAL 4:	
Complete By:	
GOAL 5:	
Complete By:	

Use time or it will use you

3a. Determine quality of life improvements

QUALITY-OF-LIFE IMPROVEMENTS (WITHIN 1 YR)	WHY THEY ARE IMPORTANT
1.	
2.	
3.	
4.	
5.	

Use time or it will use you

3b. Determine goals & milestones

GOALS (within 1 yr)	WHY THEY ARE IMPORTANT
GOAL 1: Complete By: Weekly Hours:	
GOAL 2: Complete By: Weekly Hours:	
GOAL 3: Complete By: Weekly Hours:	
GOAL 4: Complete By: Weekly Hours:	
GOAL 5: Complete By: Weekly Hours:	

4. Determine your Time Utilisation Maturity

Refer to Chapter 6 for details on how to do this.

Y/N	LEVEL 1: Chaotic
	Either no conscious long-term goals exist or, if they do, they are only vaguely formulated
	Plans, if they exist, are never written down and they are not used consistently to guide the investment and utilization of time
	No recognizable processes or techniques are used to control the investment and utilization of time
	Time is either not invested on long-term goals or, if it is, it is not invested on a regular or systematic basis
	No self-imposed deadlines or milestones are associated with tasks or long-term goals
	The majority of activities undertaken are conducted on a reactive basis
	The majority of decisions about what to do next, or of what to do at a particular time, are largely determined by others or by external factors.
	There is no on-going conscious goal-setting, or review of progress, or of goals
	No diary or related tool is used to record appointments, etc.
	Some or all of the time-wasting habits and practices identified in Appendix I and Appendix II (sections 1 and 2) are exhibited
	There is no accountability for the expenditure of time

Use time or it will use you

Y/N	LEVEL 2: Immature
	Daily and weekly goals might exist but they are not systematically written down, acted on, or reviewed on a regular basis.
	Long-term goals exist but are not written down
	Time investment on long-term goals is irregular and much less than 10% on average, per week
	Deadlines or milestones are associated with tasks but not with long-term goals
	Urgent tasks and day-to-day commitments and activities take precedence over investments of time in strategic long-term goals.
	Most time is spent on things that need to be completed within less than one week.
	Some plans exist, and are written down, but they are not consistently used to prioritize and guide the investment of time.
	To-Do lists are sometimes used to record required actions
	A diary or related tool is consistently used to record appointments, etc (+).
	Actions are predominantly driven by others and by external deadlines
	There is no regular use of prioritization.
	There is no attempt to control interruptions
	There is no attempt to measure the use of time on long-term goals
	There is no active effort to eliminate time-wasting habits and cultivate effective time-use habits.

Use time or it will use you

Y/N	LEVEL 3: Defined
	Daily, weekly and monthly plans and goals are written down and reviewed (+).
	Long term goals exist and are written down (+)
	Time investment in long-term goals is planned but not always carried out - less than 10% on average per week is invested in LTGs
	The use of time on long-term goals is measured (+)
	The time spent on things that need to be completed within less than one week no longer completely dominates.
	Recorded deadlines and milestones are associated with tasks and with long-term goals (+)
	Actions are no longer dominated by others and by external deadlines.
	There is some use of prioritization but it is not totally successful
	To-Do lists and diaries etc, are consistently used to record required actions (+)
	There are attempts to control interruptions, but they are neither completely effective, nor consistently used
	Time-wasting habits are identified and are being actively worked on
	New effectiveness habits are defined and being actively cultivated.

Use time or it will use you

Y/N	LEVEL 4: Managed
	Long, medium and short-term goal setting, review, and refinement is regularly practised (+)
	Time investment in long-term goals is planned, carried out, and measured - at least 10% of time, on average per week, is invested in LTGs (+)
	The time spent on things that need to be completed within less than one week is controlled (+)
	Interruptions are consistently and effectively controlled (+)
	Prioritization of long-term goals and other activities is regularly practiced (+)
	Task-time estimation practiced (+)
	Eighty percent of planned tasks, etc, accomplished weekly
	Ideal day performance achieved at least 80% of the time (e.g. 4 days out of 5)t
	Time-wasting habits are under control (+)
	Time-effectiveness habits actively used (+)

Y/N	LEVEL 5: Optimizing
	Long-term goals given highest priority and receiving their planned, invested time commitment, on a regular basis (every day) (+)
	Time Investment performance is running at 100% of planned for 9 out of every 10 days (+)
	Ideal Day accomplishments achieved every day (+)
	Time is invested regularly in looking for ways to improve performance and optimize processes (+)
	Analysis and measurement is used systematically to support optimizing activities (+)

Use time or it will use you

LEVEL 5: Optimizing
Long-term goals given highest priority and receiving their planned, invested time commitment on a regular basis (every day)
Time Investment performance is running at 100% of planned for 9 out of every 10 days.
Ideal Day accomplishments achieved every day
Time is invested regularly in looking for ways to improve performance and optimize processes.
Analysis and measurement is used systematically to support optimizing activities.

LEVEL 4: Managed
Long, medium and short-term goal-setting, review, and refinement is regularly practised
Time investment in long-term goals is planned and carried out and measured - at least 10% of time on average per week is invested in LTGs.
The time spent on things that need to be completed within less than one week is controlled
Interruptions are consistently and effectively controlled
Prioritization of long-term goals and other activities is regularly practised
Task-time estimation practiced
Time-wasting habits under control
Time effectiveness habits actively used

LEVEL 3: Defined
Daily, weekly and monthly plans and goals are written down and reviewed
Long-term goals exist and are written down
The use of time on long-term goals is measured
Deadlines and milestones are associated with tasks and with long-term goals.
To-Do lists and diaries etc, are consistently used to record required actions.

LEVEL 2: Immature
A diary or related tool is consistently used to record appointments, etc.

LEVEL 1: Chaotic
No consistent time utilization practices being used

Use time or it will use you

5. Determine your time-wasting habits

Y/N	MOTIVATION - PROBLEM ASSESSMENT
	Do you put off things that are important and/or things that have to be done
	Have you given up on worthwhile projects or progressed them too slowly
	Do you ever get bored.
	Do you fail to work on long-term projects consistently and therefore pay a heavy price to get oriented whenever you restart a project
	Do you have plans but not stick to them
	Do you keep putting off starting important projects
	Do you tell others you are doing the project but in fact you are doing little or nothing about it
	Do you fail to make a real commitment to important projects

Y/N	PLANNING - PROBLEM ASSESSMENT
	Do you fail to create and use weekly, monthly, yearly and longer-term plans
	Do you frequently feel busy or under pressure to get things done
	Do you fail to give highest priority to important rather than urgent things
	Do you fail to have a plan for what you are going to do each day
	Do you fail to have a clear target for what you want to accomplish in a given allocated time
	Do you fail to create and maintain a compelling set of long-term goals
	Do you fail to set and write down daily, weekly, monthly and yearly goals
	Do you fail to specifically prioritize the things you have to do
	Do you fail to review your long-term goals regularly
	Do you fail to set even a tentative deadline when you want to have each project completed.
	Do you fail to have any sort of plan for accomplishing each project
	Do you fail to breakup projects using milestones.

Use time or it will use you

6. Use your TIME-table

Y/N	TIME - WASTING HABITS ASSESSMENT
	Do you let others control too much of your use of time
	Do you frequently interrupt yourself when working on a project
	Do you respond and react to any interruption when you have planned to work on something
	Do you have a plan for each day but tend not to follow it, or not to achieve nearly as much as you had planned
	Do you avoid getting started on the main task when you begin work
	Do you work on peripheral things rather than the main task in the time allocated
	Do you overwork either all the time or fairly frequently
	Do you take longer to complete tasks than you feel is necessary
	Do you frequently let others or external events disrupt your plans
	Do you not come close (less than 80%) to achieving your weekly, monthly and yearly goals
	Do you watch the clock rather than concentrate on the task you are working on
	Do you attempt to do too many things in a day
	Do you work only one thing for too long at one stretch and become stale
	Do you fail to make best use of your time when you are fresh and have plenty of energy
	Do you try to work on long-term projects when you are tired
	Do you work on long-term projects for too short a time in one session
	Do you always stay at meetings until they finish
	Do you always answer the phone or a knock on the door
	Do you refrain from telling someone who visits that you have to start working on something else
	Do you fail to consistently measure your progress on long-term goals

Use time or it will use you

> Until you commit your goals to paper you have seeds without soil.
> Proper Planning prevents poor performance.
> What Gets Measured gets Done
> *** DON'T COMPROMISE ON PLANS. ***
> The difference between doing and dabbling is FOCUS!!!
> Set goals then take the steps to achieve them
> Value your TIME each and every day!!!

Week:

GOAL	MON	TUE	WED	THU	FRI	SAT	SUN	TOT
TOT								

EFFIC RUN %%%	MON	TUE	WED	THU	FRI	SAT	SUN	TOT
	%	%	%	%	%	%	%	%

MEETINGS+DEADLINES	WEEK GOALS
TO-DOs	**MONTH GOALS**
0	
0	
0	
0	
0	
0	
0	
0	

Appendix I: Problems with our use of time

> *I conceive that pleasures are to be avoided if greater pains be the consequence, and pains be coveted that will terminate in greater pleasures* -- Michel de Montaigne

There are a number of common problems that people have with their use of time. By asking a set of high-quality questions we can begin to understand these problems. Our individual responses may vary. What is important is that we reflect on these questions and come to our own understanding. Awareness of the origins of any problem can be an important preliminary step to solving that problem.

Why do we waste time?

Why do we waste time? In most cases we do it unintentionally. That is, if we were truly aware that we were wasting time, and we knew how to avoid doing so, we would take action.

It is important at the start to get clear what we mean by "wasting time". There are three primary ways in which we can waste time:

- by failing to spend enough time doing things that we consider important and of highest priority to us.

That is, by failing to do things which will contribute to our long-term benefit, pleasure and satisfaction.

- by taking longer to do something we want to do than is needed to complete the task.
- by doing things we do not want, or need to do, according to our value system.

Whether or not a given action or behaviour is a waste of time is a value judgement. It is not our intention here to make any judgements about exactly what activities are a waste of time. A completely satisfying and important activity for you might be regarded as a waste of time by someone else.

Clearly we have to get the balance right between doing what we want to do to meet our own needs, and doing what we need to do, to meet the needs of others. Whatever we do, we should seek to use our time effectively.

As a first step to not wasting time, we should develop the habit of being more selective and critical of what we do and how we do things. We will now look at these issues and at some of the problems that arise.

Why do we fail to plan?

Not having a clear plan how to invest time on a daily, weekly, monthly and yearly basis is probably the single most significant reason why most people do not make effective use of their time.

Use time or it will use you

If you don't have a plan on how you intend to spend your time then it is highly likely you will waste most of it.

It is very easy to verify the impact of failing to plan. Just go about your normal business for a day or even a week. At the end of each day, review and write down all the things that you accomplished and ask yourself the following questions:

- How much was done in response to the/your current situation?
- How much time was spent doing things that had to be completed within a week?
- How much time was spent doing things that did not need to be completed within a month?
- How much of your time was spent on your long-term personal goals?

When people do this sort of assessment they usually find that most, if not all, their effort goes into dealing with the current situation or with things that need to be done within the next week or month. In other words, they are operating almost completely in a reactive mode with little or no time devoted to long-term personal goals. They also discover that things that do not have to be completed for more than a week do not get much attention. In other words, they are operating in a mode where things are put off until it becomes critical to attend to them. Operating this way puts us under a lot of unnecessary stress and time pressure.

You could, as a supplementary experiment, make a written plan for a day. In this plan you should allocate a sizeable amount of time to work on several of your long-term goals and projects. These should be tasks which do not need to be completed for more than a month.

The next step is to try to faithfully execute the plan. If you are like most people you will find this very difficult to do. There will be all sorts of interruptions and things that come up on the day, that more than likely, will make it almost impossible for you to stick to your plan.

What we need to recognize is that planning gives us direction, control and focus. It changes our mode of doing things from being passive or reactive to being active. American General and President Dwight Eisenhower once made the comment: the plan is nothing, the planning is everything. This remark underlines the importance of planning but we should not interpret it in a way that undervalues the importance of what goes into a plan.

Prioritisation and planning needs to be done in advance and plans should always be written down. Planning should be done on a daily, weekly monthly and yearly basis. A plan should prioritize what we are going to do and, for each task, it should include details of when we are going to start and when we expect to finish and what we intend to accomplish. Such plans need to be frequently reviewed. Without a plan there is a strong chance that important things will either get put off, or forgotten altogether.

Use time or it will use you

Why do we put things off?

Procrastination, or putting things off, is something that each and every one of us does. There are three kinds of putting off:

- putting off things we have to do,
- putting off things we would like to, or think we should do, and
- putting off things that we do not place a high priority upon.

Procrastination is the thief of time -- Edward Young

It is useful to be aware of potential causes of procrastination. There are clearly many reasons why people put things off. If our current level of

. pleasure or satisfaction is higher than what we judge will be derived from doing the task or project then there is likely to be little motivation for doing it. However, this level of decision-making is not usually the best guide for putting things off.

There are times when we keep putting something off which we must do or which we don't want to put off and which we are committed to achieving. This situation can be serious. There are several common reasons for putting off things we want to, or have to, do:

- *we don't know where to start or how to tackle the task.* We either consciously or unconsciously hope that by delaying the task we will be better placed to tackle it at some later time. Our hope is that additional information will become available that will clarify or make the task easier. This position can only be justified if we are actively seeking to improve our preparedness to tackle the task.

- *we are uncertain about the outcome or consequences of performing the task or taking the necessary action.* There may be a risk or a fear of failure or rejection. Fear of failure is not a good basis for putting off something. There are rarely absolute guarantees with anything that we do. In this situation, we need to rationalize our position. If, according to our values and circumstances, the task must be performed then we are committed to it, whatever the outcome. There are then only two justifiable actions in these circumstances:

    o to reassess our commitment to the task. This should include assessing the consequences and cost of delaying taking action. At the outset of the reassessment we should make the commitment that, depending on our findings, we will either take action or abandon the task.

    o to make preparations to cope with the uncertainty, whatever it may be, and then take action,

- *we assess that undertaking the task/action will be emotionally or physically painful to us and/or to others.* Putting things off in these circumstances, either from our own perspective or from that of others, is hardly ever justifiable. In our own case, it may lead to anguish and worry which will distract and stop us being effective with the other things we are currently doing.

- *taking the action may go against our core beliefs.* In this situation our only way forward is to reassess both our core beliefs and the cost of not performing the action. Our core values should be the final arbiter. However these values should be weighed against those upheld by a fair, a caring and a just society.

Putting off something that we judge is not a high priority is always fair enough. However it is best not to leave things "up in the air". Having taken the trouble to give something a down-graded priority we should take the matter one step further. That is, we should ask ourselves if we ever intend to carry out the task in the foreseeable future. If we do, then we should set a dead-line for when we intend to complete the task, otherwise we should strike it off our list of things to do. It is important to be decisive about this if we want to rid ourselves of procrastination and indecision. Putting a deadline on things influences our behaviour. It underlines our commitment to the task. What remains is to allocate our priorities to honour that commitment.

Putting off things we would "like" to do is always problematic. To be fair to our own growth as a person we should invest the extra effort with such things to move them from the "like to" category either to the "have to" category or to a category "going to". The latter is not highest priority but there is a dead-line, and a commitment to achieving such things.

Why do we always feel busy?

Because they are always doing things, and because there is always a pile of other things still to do, a lot of people think they are constantly busy. They use this situation to legitimise their behaviour and to explain to themselves, and others, why, seemingly important tasks, are not accomplished.

If we are to be effective we have to face up to the fact that there will always be more things we could do than we physically have time for. Given that this is the way the world is, we should see that attempting to do more than we are able to accomplish is not the best way to live our lives and gain pleasure and satisfaction from what we do.

People who say they are always busy rarely accomplish very much from which they can derive long-lasting pleasure and satisfaction.

Clearly, it is what we give priority to, that will make a difference to our lives. Everyone gives priority to things -that is, they make choices about what to do all the time. However, most of these choices are not governed by a prioritization that is likely to lead to long-lasting satisfaction and pleasure. Instead, the choice of what to do now, and what to do next, is often whimsical or without consistency, coherence or overall direction.

The fundamental reason many people end up feeling busy most of the time is because they spend far too much of their time attending to things that need to be done in the immediate short-term -this hour, this day, or this week. We need to plan and shift our effort so that as much as possible of whatever we are doing is not just reactive to the current situation. Doing something that is going to take half a day (which you knew about three weeks ago) on the day it is due, is just giving yourself unnecessary stress. lust-in-time management might work for stock-control in warehouses, but it is not an effective way to conduct your affairs. There are some people, like staff who work in the emergency section of a hospital, who do get genuinely busy. However, most busyness is self-imposed and avoidable with proper planning, with knowing what is important long-term, and by use of effective time-skills. Even people who are genuinely busy, who wish to work on long-term goals, can usually, through agreement with others, or with their boss, or by improving their processes in a creative way, find some quality time to work on long-term goals. Whenever you are busy, study the process you are using -almost always, there are ways within your reach to make it more effective and thereby save time that can be invested in long-term activities.

Why do we overwork?

Overwork is a form of wasting time because it involves the ineffective use of time. How often do you hear people say they are so busy they have to work sixteen or even eighteen hour days. It may sometimes be necessary to do this sort of thing for short periods but it is folly to do it for any extended time period. For some people, such behaviour is an "ego-trip" or an exercise in self-indulgence and self-importance. They gain pleasure from boasting to others about how hard they work. More often than not, these claims are an exaggeration. Or, what people classify as "work", has very little to do with work, or with achieving worthwhile goals.

Anyone who indulges in this behaviour, or who is forced to do this, should reassess their situation. The goal should always be, not to spend say 16 hours working (or at work) each day, but instead to make progress and get the job done. It is easy enough to spend 12 or 16 hours at your work, but to use 12 or 16 hours in a day working effectively is something a world apart.

It is very unlikely that anyone who spends long hours each day "working" on their job or on some project is being effective. Such behaviour is symptomatic of poor prioritization and lack of ability to effectively use time.

We cannot live in a family or in a relationship, or work in an organization and devote all or most of our time (or even all of our spare time) to working on the things which we judge to be of highest priority for us alone. If we attempt to do this then life will become intolerable, if not for ourselves, for those around us. Such behaviour is obsessive and unlikely to lead to lasting pleasure or satisfaction. Each and everyone of us can however use our time more effectively to our own benefit, and to the benefit of those around us. In the end, it comes down to setting and committing to priorities and achieving a balance in how we spend our time.

Why don't we give important things highest priority?

Most people acquire a lot of their behaviours and values from what they see going on around them. When we look around us, it is very unlikely we will see many, if any, examples of people who consistently make effective use of their time. Instead, we will see people everywhere going about their business letting their environment largely control what they do, and when they do it. Because this is the norm, and this is what we are usually surrounded by, most of us never even consider that there might be a better alternative.

What this means is that most of us are passive rather than active users of time. That is, we spend most of our time in reactive mode or in a mode that we consider to be dictated by our circumstances. In other words, we exercise very little control over what we do, when we do things, and how long we spend doing any particular thing.

When it comes to time utilization, and choosing how to use our time, many of us seem to conform to Parkinson's famous law.

The time devoted to things is usually inversely proportional to their importance -- C. N. Parkinson

Most of us have at least some idea of what it would be important for us to do if we were to become successful in our own terms. However, as Parkinson's Law suggests, people rarely put much time into things that are important, even by their own standards.

Is this because people do not want to be successful, and do not want to achieve long-lasting pleasure and satisfaction from . what they accomplish? This seems hardly likely.

There are however three things that prevent us doing things that we consider important:

- the things we consider "important" do not provide us with enough motivation to want to take action to achieve them. Or, as motivation coach Anthony Robbins would say, we have 'impotent goals'.
- we don't think we can achieve the things that we consider important or desirable.
- we are not willing to pay the price. That is, we are not willing to invest the time to achieve the things that we consider important.

None of these reasons, for not spending more time on important long-term projects is excusable or defensible. Only by becoming much more discriminating, and by exercising much greater control over the way we use our time, will we have the chance to become much more effective time users. We must reject most of what we see going on around us as exemplars of how to make effective use of our time.

In summary, we will not make progress in getting done things that we consider important until we consciously and actively exercise much greater control over our use of time, no matter what our current circumstances are. We need to plan, to identify what is important to us, to set our priorities, to make commitments and to follow through on our plans with never a thought of giving up. Everyone of us can do this. What it requires is that we take action, today, tomorrow, every day!

Why do we take too long to complete tasks?

Every task only needs a finite amount of time and effort to complete it. It is therefore a rational and desirable objective not to spend more time on a task than is needed. However most of the time, this is not what happens. We end up taking a lot longer to complete tasks than what is really needed.

For tasks that have to be completed by a certain time, or within a given time, a very common behaviour is that all the time that is available is used. Once again a law due to Parkinson captures this succinctly.

The work expands to fit the time available -- C.N. Parkinson

In his discussion of this law in operation, Parkinson cites the story of an elderly lady of leisure who spends the entire day carrying out the task of writing and posting a postcard to her niece: an hour spent finding the postcard, another searching for her spectacles, an hour and a quarter composing the letter, twenty minutes deciding whether to take an umbrella when going out to post the postcard, and so on. In the end, the lady is left prostrate and exhausted after a day of doubt, anxiety and toil.

Parkinson goes on to suggest that the same task might not occupy a busy person for more than three minutes. The message is clear!

The behaviour of letting tasks expand to fill the time available certainly does not correspond to the effective use of time. When it happens the value that is dominating is that the task has to be completed by such and such a time, I will therefore pace myself to complete the task in the allotted time. To avoid this behaviour we need to put Parkinson's law to work for us, and against what it stands for.

For task completion, a far more empowering value would be: I should not spend any longer on a task than is absolutely necessary to do the job properly and complete it. Hence, it is important to set firm and realistic targets which define when tasks should be completed.

Before leaving this discussion, it is worthwhile pointing out that Parkinson's law is just a special case of a far more general law that applies to the use of resources.

People individually, and in organizations, adjust their behaviour to utilize all that is available of any desirable finite resource, no matter what the real needs of the situation.

This law would appear to apply to everything from watching television, to eating food on our plates or in our refrigerators, to spending money, to utilizing office space, to the utilization of available disk space on our computer systems. There are very few resource situations where this law does not seem to apply.

We need to keep this law in mind, not only in relation to time utilization, but also in relation to lots of other things that impact the quality of our lives. What this law tells us is that people, by and large, tend to follow the path of least resistance or find the easiest way to deal with any given situation. While looking for easier ways to do things, or to respond to situations, is a powerful form of optimizing, it can also lead to unnecessary waste of resources and time, if abused.

To finish off this section let us now examine what commonly happens with projects that have deadlines and others that are longer term with no fixed time for completion.

Behaviour for Projects With Deadlines:

A common behaviour that people exhibit with projects that have a deadline is that they put things off and end up having to rush at the end to finish by the requisite time. There are several risks with this strategy.

Our estimate of how long it will take to complete the task is a serious underestimate. There can also be a real problem if something unexpected goes wrong or something else also needs to be attended to urgently. Finally, because of the time pressure, we are much more likely to make mistakes and hence the quality of what we do will suffer.

Long-term Projects

For long-term projects things are even worse. Such projects rarely have a deadline and our ability to estimate how long they will take is usually very poor. As a result there is a very high risk that a long-term project will end up taking a lot longer to complete than it should have. Or, the project will end up being abandoned after substantial effort has been invested. Some common time-wasting and stalling behaviours that many of us exhibit for large projects include:

- we keep putting off starting the project
- we tell others we are doing the project but in fact we are doing little or nothing about it
- we fail to make a real commitment to the project.
- we fail to set even a tentative deadline when we want to have the project complete.
- we fail to have any sort of plan for accomplishing the project
- we fail to break the project up using milestones.

Why do people give up on worthwhile projects?

It is a common occurrence for someone to start out with enthusiasm on a long-term project only to stall and give it up part of the way through. Occasionally there are things that happen beyond our control, that justifiably bring worthwhile projects to a halt. More often than not, however, worthwhile projects are abandoned because people lose their momentum and commitment to the project.

Use time or it will use you

There are several negative consequences that flow from giving up on long-term, worthwhile projects. They include:

- loss of our investment of time
- an undermining of our confidence in our ability to complete such projects
- a perception by others that we do not have the ability to follow through on worthwhile projects
- a loss of what we would have gained from completing the project

These are consequences we should give serious consideration to before embarking on any large project in the first place. Also, these are things we should always carefully reconsider and weigh up before ever abandoning any long-term project.

There are lots of things that can undermine the completion of a long-term project. We should be aware of these at the outset and have a plan for ensuring that they do not interfere with our project. They include:

- failing to have a clear idea of what we are trying to achieve
- failing to have our heart in the project from the outset
- failing to allocate and invest enough time on a regular basis
- failing to set tangible milestones and deadlines that allow us to see and measure regular progress

- letting other projects/activities distract us and use up our available time
- letting problems, (technical, conceptual or otherwise) with the project itself defeat us
- letting others, or unanticipated external events undermine our efforts
- getting caught up in the perpetual "it's almost finished" syndrome
- being inflexible and unable to adapt to the real needs of the project
- being too impatient for results.

If we are realistic, we must recognize that with any large project there are always going to be flat spots along the way where we have doubts about whether it is worth continuing with the project. This is normal and natural with any large undertaking. However, provided we have properly prepared for these problems in the first place they will not sink the project. It is just like going on a long camping trek. We make a number of contingency plans at the outset so that if something goes wrong we are not totally surprised or overwhelmed. Instead we are equipped to meet the challenge and continue to make progress. Later we will see the sort of precautions we can take to ensure that our important projects don't get sunk or just wither away and die a slow death.

Why do we get bored?

People who are bored are very vulnerable to wasting their time. How often do you hear someone say "they are bored". This has to be one of the greatest indictments of modern society . We live in a world of such richness and diversity and yet there are so many people who frequently complain of being bored.

How can this possibly happen? What can we do about it so that it never happens again?

Living is a gift. Each one of us has the chance to live each and every day to the full. The problem is many people do not take much responsibility for living. They expect others to provide what will prevent them from being bored. They are passive rather than active livers of life. They wait for someone else to organize their time.

When someone announces that "they are bored" we need to ask what is the motive behind making such a statement. These motives usually fall into one of three categories:

- More often than not they want someone else to do something for them, to take the initiative. For example, they want someone to suggest "let's go to a movie" or go out to dinner, or to some other distraction that will entertain them or give them their fix of transitory pleasure.

- Alternatively, they may be doing something which they don't want to have to continue doing. In this case, by their announcement, they want someone else to say "alright, you don't have to keep doing that -you can do something else if you want to".

- A third reason for someone saying that they are bored is really an indirect way of saying to their listener that they are not very happy with the way things are. And, they want the person they announce this to, to do something about it.

So when we, or someone close to us, announces that they are bored we need to be aware of what is really going on, so that we can do something constructive about it. Clearly, each of these different types of boredom needs to be handled differently.

While there are some people who are very susceptible to being bored, there are another group of people who never feel or announce that they are bored. Why is this so? If we were to question the two groups we would most probably find that the set of core values that they had were quite different.

People who never get bored have developed compelling interests that they enjoy or gain pleasure and satisfaction from. They have plenty of self-esteem and a strong sense of purpose. They have goals and they think about the long-term as well as about what happens today. In fact they are prepared to invest time doing things today which will only have payoffs in the future. Acquiring these values is not something that costs money. It comes down to making a commitment to improve the quality of your life and to take ACTION to do something about it.

Can we be happy doing "nothing"?

Some people believe or act as though they can be happy doing nothing. By "doing nothing" I mean living a life without ambition, based on routine, on passive action and on responding to whatever life puts before them. Most of the so-called "mid-life crises" people have, can probably be traced back to their coming to the realization that they are living their life this way.

Certainly, there is no law that says we should not live without ambition. However, if everyone took this attitude there would be little progress in human affairs. A person, by doing nothing, by not developing their full potential is taking from society, but not giving anything in return.

Most of us have a need to seek pleasure and satisfaction. Therefore by doing nothing, we are short-changing ourselves, those around us, and society at large. Living this way, it is unlikely that we will ever experience anything other than a very shallow and unsatisfying form of happiness. This would seem to be a selfish, naive, thoughtless, unfulfilling and futile way to live. Life offers us a great opportunity, we should not waste or squander it.

In choosing how to live, and how to use our time we should not necessarily set our standards by what others do. This in no way, however, precludes learning from the best of what others have to teach us. Throughout history, and around us today, there are numerous shining examples of how life has been, and can be, lived. These are the benchmarks by which we should judge our own actions.

Use time or it will use you

We should seek to live life to the full according to our own particular values, and aspirations. When we are old, we should be able to look back on what we have achieved and not see just a barren wasteland of squandered opportunity.

Life is a daring adventure -or nothing! Helen Keller

Appendix II: The psychology of time utilization

Only a man who marches far appreciates the sweetness of the water at his journey's end -- G. Johnston

What influences our behaviour?

Gaining some understanding of what lies behind our behavior is useful if we are to significantly change the way we utilize time. Exactly what motivates behaviour is always highly personal. It is based upon, or at least it is influenced by, our current set of personal values, our beliefs, our experiences and the habits we have developed, or allowed to form.

Most of the things that we do, and the way we spend our time, can be explained in terms of the moral, social, cultural and political influences in our past and present personal environment. There are also broader community, national and global influences which can temper what we do. On top of all this, is each individual's own original synthesis or selection of values and beliefs. This whole melting pot, while it contains some elements of stability based on core values, is constantly changing at the edges as a result of new experiences. It is from all these influences that we learn what is acceptable, what is desirable, and what is workable for us as individuals living in relationships and functioning in society. This all in turn influences what we do to seek pleasure, to seek satisfaction and to avoid pain.

Our behaviour, and hence what we do, is strongly influenced by our current values, beliefs, experiences and habits.

It is convenient to imagine that there is a pyramid of influences that govern what we choose to do. At the top of the pyramid is a relatively small set of intangible, relatively stable core values that we subscribe to. We use these as loose guiding principles for what we do. They influence our behaviour to some degree but are by no means absolute predictors of behaviour.

We may think of these core values as high-level beliefs. In some cases core values appear to be formed before their supporting beliefs, while in other instances, a set of beliefs may lead to the formation of a core value. In the latter case they are generalizations or abstractions derived from a coherent or consistent set of beliefs. Core values sometimes act as filters for the beliefs we adopt.

```
          /\
         /  \
        /Core\
       /Values\
      /--------\
     /  Labels  \
    /------------\
   /   Beliefs    \
  /----------------\
 /      Habits      \
/--------------------\
/Events and Experiences\
------------------------
```

An example of a core value might be something like "I like to do things properly". Just where we draw the line between core values and supporting beliefs is difficult to determine. For our purposes it is not all that important.

Sitting below our core values in the pyramid are a set of supporting beliefs. These beliefs are of two kinds: labels that pertain to ourselves and more specific beliefs. Labels are things that we give ourselves and that others also give us. They usually imply a whole series of values, behaviours and capabilities that are commonly associated with each label. Examples are things like "I am a scientist", or "I am a Buddhist" or "I am Swedish" or "I am a good swimmer", etc.

The beliefs that sit below the labels tend to be more tangible and hence more suitable as a basis for personal decision-making and influencing our behaviour. They are statements that often can be shown to be either right or wrong, or true or false in a given context. Examples are things like: "I put on weight if I have a lot of ice cream and soft drinks". Our values influence the set of labels and beliefs we hold and vice versa although sometimes there are inconsistencies in our beliefs and between our beliefs and our values. Our beliefs, and to a lesser extent, the values we hold, influence our behaviour. What we do however, when familiar situations or preconditions apply, is largely governed by habit.

Habits are abstractions of repeatable and reusable behaviour. If we look at what we do in a day, or in a week, then we will see that much of it is based on habit. Habits are formed in all sorts of ways. Often we learn habits from observing or conforming to what others do. In other cases, we do something seemingly by chance and derive some success, benefit, pleasure or satisfaction from doing it. This experience may be enough to lead to the formation of a habit. There are also occasions when we must take action in unfamiliar situations. Then, for guidance, we revert to looser higher-level knowledge, or we respond intuitively or instinctively. This is when we "grow" and form new behaviours, new habits and occasionally even new values. Here our core values and supporting beliefs can have some influence over the habits we form, although once again, there can be inconsistencies.

Once a habit is formed it is usually used thereafter without ever seriously questioning whether it is a good or an efficient habit. We rely on the use of habits a lot because they save us having to think about how we should respond in familiar situations. Habits are therefore much more reliable predictors of behaviour than beliefs or values. • They reduce stress by delivering predictable outcomes and by minimizing our need to actively think in familiar situations.

The large number of actions we take accumulate as experiences that form the base of our pyramid of influence. They are manifestations of, and instances of, behaviour. In familiar situations our actions are, more often than not, governed by habit or past experiences. In unfamiliar situations we revert to our beliefs, labels or even our values for guidance on how we should behave.

This model is an oversimplification of reality. It is not a scholarly proposal derived from years of psychological study. However the chain of dependencies it provides can give us at least some insight into how we decide what we will do.

values-> labels->beliefs ->habits->experiences->actions

The example below illustrates an application of the model and the relationships between the different layers of the pyramid. There are often a number of labels and beliefs, etc which influence a particular behaviour.

Example:
```
    Value:   I like to keep fit (not true or false)
    Label:   I am health-conscious
    Belief:  I need to run for 30 minutes four times a week to keep
             aerobically fit (statement - can be true or false)
    Habit:   I run on Mondays, Wednesdays, Saturdays and Sundays
             (abstracted behaviour)
    Action:  I ran on last Monday evening (instance)
```

Understanding all the subtleties of what motivates human behaviour is a task of enormous scope. We will not attempt to come to terms with all the relationships and interactions. Instead what we will try to do is focus more directly on beliefs and behaviours that impact our effective use of time. In doing this we fully acknowledge that each person might arrive at a given behaviour from quite a different set of values, beliefs and habits.

If we want to change a behaviour that impacts our use of time then becoming conscious of values, labels, beliefs and habits that influence this behaviour is an advantage.

It is easier to change behaviour when you understand what its cause is.

A sample list of traits, values and beliefs that can undermine our effective use of time are:

- some people prefer to be "entertained" at every opportunity
- some people are "happy" doing nothing
- some people prefer no one, including themselves, governing how they spend their time
- some people have only a weak commitment to priorities
- some people are inconsistent in relation to time - they say one thing and do another
- some people go through the motions but without involvement
- some people perceive that they are constantly busy
- some people believe they should only work on long-term goals when there is time
- some people are frequently bored
- some people have no sense of time

It is from values, beliefs and traits like this sample set that people form their poor time habits and behaviours.

The role of habits in time utilization

As we have already seen habits are a natural mechanism that human beings use to "cope" with the large number of situations they encounter when they go about their daily business. Habits are essentially situation action rules. That is, we have stored in our mind hundreds of rules of the form:

if situation XX applies then take action YY

Our consciousness constantly monitors what situation we are in. If we are in a familiar situation then, more than likely, we will have a readily defined action to apply. For example, the first thing you might do when you come home from work is to switch on the TV. If this is one of the habits you have formed then, more than likely, when you come home on any given day this is what you will automatically or almost compulsively do, without a second thought.

The chains of habit are too weak to be felt until they are too strong to be broken. Samuel Johnson

Why do people (and animals too) have such a strong tendency to form habits? The reason would seem to be pretty clear. Most people have a strong desire for predictability and "being in control" of their situation no matter what the circumstances. Whenever we are not "in control" there is uncertainty both about what to do and what might be the outcome . And, we have learned that uncertainty can mean inconvenience, threat, stress and possibly psychological or physical pain.

Of course, in many circumstances, habits are very useful and necessary. However, from a time perspective, there are two issues:

- the first is that we want to be sure that we do not have many habits that are time-wasters, and
- the second is that we want to use our natural tendency to form habits to design new habits that will empower us to invest and make more effective use of our time.

Each of us has our own bag full of time-wasting habits. Often we are not even conscious that we have such habits. An important step towards improving our use of time is to develop one more habit -that of becoming conscious of the way we do things from an effectiveness perspective. The following are a sample list of common time-wasting habits.

- letting others control too much of the use of our time
- frequently interrupting ourselves when working on a project
- responding and reacting to any interruption when we have planned to work on something
- failing to have a plan for what we are going to do each day
- failing to have a clear target for what we want to accomplish in a given allocated time
- failing to work on long-term projects consistently and therefore paying a heavy price to get oriented whenever we restart on a project
- avoiding getting started on the main task when we begin work
- working on peripheral things rather than the main task in the time allocated
- failing to create and maintain a compelling set of long-term goals
- failing to set and write down daily, weekly, monthly and yearly goals
- watching the clock rather than concentrating on the task and being committed to it.

- attempting to do too many things in a day
- doing only one thing for too long a time and becoming stale
- failing to make best use of our time when we are fresh and have plenty of energy
- failing to specifically prioritize the things we have to do
- having a plan but not sticking to it
- trying to work on long-term projects when we are tired
- working on long-term projects for too short a time in one session
- always staying at meetings until they finish
- always answering the phone or a knock on the door
- not telling someone who visits that we have to start working on something else
- failing to review our long-term goals regularly
- failing to measure our progress on long-term goals

Curing these bad habits, in most cases, leads directly to the formation of good habits.

Influences working against our effective use of time

Our broader social environment, and the norms and behaviour of society at large, also have a strong influence on how we behave and how we utilize time.

An implicit underlying assumption of present-day societies is that they work better and they are easier to govern/control when their is a high degree of conformance and uniformity in the behaviour of individuals. If, for example, this was not the case, how would we get the majority of people to pay their taxes or refrain from going through red lights, etc, etc, etc.

A second implicit assumption of societies is that the larger the population in a given society, the more conformance and the greater the number of rules/laws that are needed for the society to function for the common good.

The pressures for conformance are imposed on us from all quarters: our family, our friends and peers, the school, the workplace, sporting teams,

religious congregations and other social groups that we participate in. Each has it own set of norms, values and shared beliefs that propagate conformance.

Most free-thinking people who take the time to think about this whole issue are likely to conclude that we all have to pay the price of a reasonably high degree of conformance, if we are to obtain the "benefits" that an organized society can deliver.

If we assume that the price, a high degree of conformity, has to be paid for society to work, then we have to live with its consequences. A major impact of most conforming influences is to induce a large dose of PASSIVITY, reactive behaviour and inaction into the majority of individuals. The people who govern/control society at various levels see a high degree of passivity among their constituents as a good thing. It makes their job simpler and it allows them to more easily achieve their objectives (these objectives are not always solely associated with the common good).

Unfortunately, the cloud of passivity-inducing influences that rains down on us as individuals is a great enemy of our efforts to use time strategically to improve the quality of our lives. For, it is only through large amounts of sustained action, and not passivity, that we achieve worthwhile accomplishments that will give us long-lasting pleasure and satisfaction. This is the issue that we, as individuals, must comprehend, confront and transcend if we are to derive the benefits that using our time wisely and strategically can deliver. The various societies that we participate in only encourage conforming actions -this is the reality that surrounds us. We must not expect our social environment to be very sympathetic or supportive of our efforts to make better use of our time.

To get a clearer grasp of what we are trying to convey here, let us consider the case of sport. In relative terms, only a small proportion of the population actively participate in playing a given sport. A much larger number of people take the relatively passive action of going to venues to watch the sport. And, a much larger number of people still, take the even more passive action of sitting at home in front of their

TV s watching the sport being played. This sort of scenario is repeated over and over throughout society. In each case, there are a small number of doers who are taking the action and getting the benefits. The vast majority sit back and watch it happen without contributing much that will either benefit society or give them long-lasting pleasure and satisfaction. In making these comments we are not saying that passive interests are bad or that we should not participate in passive interests. What we are suggesting is that is we need to balance our passive interests with other interests where we clearly take the role of being doers.

An appreciation that these more pervasive influences exist, and are working against our efforts to take action, can help. We need to acknowledge that they exist and begin to take the necessary countermeasures that will dissipate their influence on our efforts.

Influences encouraging us to use our time effectively

Not all the broader influences in society work against our efforts to use our time strategically and effectively. Society, through its institutions, the media and other channels, values, recognizes and rewards those who demonstrate sustained commitment to achieve long-term and worthy goals in education, sport, business, science, the arts and elsewhere. Examples of this recognition may be enough to encourage at least some people to set out to achieve worthy long-term goals. Unfortunately, in most cases, this is where society's encouragement to individuals stops.

Where society lets us down is that it is virtually silent on informing us that the greatest pleasure and satisfaction in life comes from accomplishment. Those people who have worked long and hard to complete a project or achieve a goal appreciate this. Unfortunately many people never experience this sort of satisfaction and are therefore not motivated to even attempt any long-term projects that could make a real difference to the quality of their lives. Others attempt worthy projects, but because of their lack of time and the other barriers that society puts in the way, give up. Only the most persistent achieve long-term goals ¬this does not have to happen. With better know ledge and better time skills we should be able to substantially increase our success rate on achieving long-term goals.

The way ahead

Each and every one of us, owes it to themselves, at least once in our life, to tackle and complete a project that is going to require a large investment of time and effort. To do this we need to have access to an abundance of time. And, once we have that time, we need to use it strategically and effectively.

To learn how to use time strategically and effectively three things are necessary:

- we must have an understanding the underlying causes of poor time utilisation
- we must have a number of tactics for effective time utilisation

- but, to be truly successful, the first two sets of requirements must be underpinned by a perspective or philosophy built upon a set of guiding principles from which all else follows

Chapters 2 and 3 spell out those guiding principles. We have chosen to separate these principles into two broadly based categories: those that could loosely be characterized as describing what to, and what not to invest time in and those describing how to and how not to go about investing our time. The latter set, which are more pragmatic rather than philosophic or strategic, are discussed in chapter 3.

The two sets of laws that are proposed are largely coherent and cohesive. That is, they are constructively reinforcing. What we mean by this is that to derive maximum benefit from their use as guiding principles we should always try to bring to bear as many of them as possible in any given situation where time investment or time utilization is involved.

The End